# SCHAUM'S *Easy* OUTLINES

# PRECALCULUS

# Other Books in Schaum's Easy Outlines Series Include:

Schaum's Easy Outlines: College Mathematics
Schaum's Easy Outlines: College Algebra
Schaum's Easy Outlines: Calculus
Schaum's Easy Outlines: Elementary Algebra
Schaum's Easy Outlines: Mathematical Handbook
   of Formulas and Tables
Schaum's Easy  Outlines: Geometry
Schaum's Easy Outlines: Trigonometry
Schaum's Easy  Outlines: Probability and Statistics
Schaum's Easy Outlines: Statistics
Schaum's Easy Outlines: Principles of Accounting
Schaum's Easy Outlines: Biology
Schaum's Easy Outlines: College Chemistry
Schaum's Easy Outlines: Genetics
Schaum's Easy Outlines: Human Anatomy
   and Physiology
Schaum's Easy Outlines: Organic Chemistry
Schaum's Easy Outlines: Physics
Schaum's Easy Outlines: Basic Electricity
Schaum's Easy Outlines: Programming with C++
Schaum's Easy Outlines: Programming with Java
Schaum's Easy Outlines: French
Schaum's Easy Outlines: German
Schaum's Easy Outlines: Spanish
Schaum's Easy Outlines: Writing and Grammar

SCHAUM'S *Easy* OUTLINES

# PRECALCULUS

BASED ON SCHAUM'S *Outline of Precalculus*
BY FRED SAFIER

ABRIDGEMENT EDITOR:
KIMBERLY S. KIRKPATRICK

## SCHAUM'S OUTLINE SERIES
### McGRAW-HILL

New York   Chicago   San Francisco   Lisbon   London   Madrid
Mexico City   Milan   New Delhi   San Juan
Seoul   Singapore   Sydney   Toronto

**FRED SAFIER** teaches mathematics at the City College of San Francisco and is the author of numerous students' solution manuals in algebra, trigonometry, and precalculus. He received an A.B. in Physics from Harvard College and an M.S. in Mathematics from Stanford University.

**KIMBERLY S. KIRKPATRICK** teaches mathematics at Transylvania University in Lexington, Kentucky. She earned a B.S. in Mathematics Education, a Master of Applied Mathematics, and a Ph.D. in Mathematics, all from Auburn University. She is the co-author of professional papers and previously taught at the University of Evansville.

1 2 3 4 5 6 7 8 9 DOC/DOC 0 9 8 7 6 5 4 3 2

ISBN 0-07-138340-9

*McGraw-Hill*

*A Division of The McGraw·Hill Companies*

# Contents

Chapter 1    Number Systems, Polynomials,
             and Exponents                            1
Chapter 2    Equations and Inequalities              13
Chapter 3    Systems of Equations and
             Partial Fractions                       27
Chapter 4    Analytic Geometry and Functions         39
Chapter 5    Algebraic Functions and
             Their Graphs                             54
Chapter 6    Exponential and
             Logarithmic Functions                   71
Chapter 7    Conic Sections                          78
Chapter 8    Trigonometric Functions                 87
Chapter 9    Trigonometric Identities and
             Trigonometric Inverses                  104
Chapter 10   Sequences and Series                    116
Index                                                121

# Chapter 1
# NUMBER SYSTEMS, POLYNOMIALS, AND EXPONENTS

IN THIS CHAPTER:

- ✔ *Sets of Numbers*
- ✔ *Axioms for the Real Number System*
- ✔ *Properties of Inequalities*
- ✔ *Absolute Value*
- ✔ *Complex Numbers*
- ✔ *Order of Operations*
- ✔ *Polynomials*
- ✔ *Factoring*
- ✔ *Exponents*
- ✔ *Rational and Radical Expressions*

## Sets of Numbers

The sets of numbers used in algebra are, in general, subsets of $R$, the set of *real numbers*.

- *Natural numbers* $N$: The counting numbers, e.g., 1, 2, 3, …
- *Integers* $Z$: The counting numbers, together with their opposites and 0, e.g., 0, 1, 2, 3, …, −1, −2, −3…

- *Rational Numbers $Q$*: The set of all numbers that can be written as quotients $a/b$, $b \neq 0$, $a$ and $b$ integers, e.g., $3/17$, $-5/13$, …
- *Irrational Numbers $H$*: All real numbers that are not rational numbers, e.g., $\pi$, $\sqrt{2}$, $\sqrt[3]{5}$, $-\pi/3$, …

**Example 1.1:** The number $-5$ is a member of the sets $Z$, $Q$, $R$. The number $156.73$ is a member of the sets $Q$, $R$. The number $5\pi$ is a member of the sets $H$, $R$.

# Axioms for the Real Number System

There are two fundamental operations, addition and multiplication, which have the following properties ($a$, $b$, $c$ arbitrary real numbers):

- *Commutative Laws* :
    $a + b = b + a$: order does not matter in addition.
    $ab = ba$: order does not matter in multiplication.
- *Associative Laws*:
    $a + (b + c) = (a + b) + c$: grouping does not matter in repeated addition.
    $a(bc) = (ab)c$: grouping does not matter in repeated multiplication.
- *Distributive Laws*:
    $a(b + c) = ab + ac$; also $(a + b)c = ac + bc$: multiplication is distributive over addition.
- *Zero Factor Laws*:
    For every real number $a$, $a \cdot 0 = 0$.
    If $ab = 0$, then either $a = 0$ or $b = 0$.
- *Laws for Negatives:*
    $-(-a) = a$
    $(-a)(-b) = ab$
    $-ab = (-a)b = a(-b) = -(-a)(-b) = -(ab)$
    $(-1)a = -a$
- *Laws for Quotients:*
    $$-\frac{a}{b} = \frac{-a}{b} = \frac{a}{-b} = -\frac{-a}{-b}$$

    $$\frac{-a}{-b} = \frac{a}{b}$$

    $$\frac{a}{b} = \frac{c}{d} \text{ if and only if } ad = bc.$$

$$\frac{a}{b} = \frac{ka}{kb}, \text{ for } k \text{ any nonzero real number.}$$

## Properties of Inequalities

The number $a$ *is less than* $b$, written $a < b$, if $b - a$ is positive. If $a < b$ then $b$ *is greater than* $a$, written $b > a$. If $a$ is either less than or equal to $b$, this is written $a \leq b$. If $a \leq b$ then $b$ is greater than or equal to $a$, written $b \geq a$.

The following properties may be deduced from these definitions:

- If $a < b$, then $a + c < b + c$.

- If $a < b$, then $\begin{cases} ac < bc \text{ if } c > 0 \\ ac > bc \text{ if } c < 0. \end{cases}$

- If $a < b$ and $b < c$, then $a < c$.

## Absolute Value

The *absolute value* of a real number $a$, written $|a|$, is defined as follows:

$$|a| = \begin{cases} a \text{ if } a \geq 0 \\ -a \text{ if } a < 0. \end{cases}$$

## Complex Numbers

Not all numbers are real numbers. The set of complex numbers, $C$, contains all numbers of the *standard form* $a + bi$, where $a$ and $b$ are real and $i^2 = -1$. Since every real number $x$ can be written as $x + 0i$, it follows that every real number is also a complex number. The complex numbers that are *not* real are sometimes known as *imaginary numbers*.

**Example 1.2:** $3 + \sqrt{-4} = 3 + 2i, \ -5i, \ 2\pi i, \ \dfrac{1}{2} + \dfrac{\sqrt{3}}{2}i$ are examples of complex (imaginary) numbers.

In standard form, complex numbers can be combined using the operations defined for real numbers, together with the definition of the imaginary unit $i$: $i^2 = -1$. The conjugate of a complex number $z$ is denoted $\bar{z}$. If $z = a + bi$, then $\bar{z} = a - bi$.

## Order of Operations

In expressions involving combinations of operations, the following order is observed:

1. Perform operations within grouping symbols first. If grouping symbols are nested inside other grouping symbols, proceed from the innermost outward.
2. Apply exponents before performing multiplications and divisions, unless grouping symbols indicate otherwise.
3. Perform multiplications and divisions, in order from left to right, before performing additions and subtractions (also from left to right), unless operation symbols indicate otherwise.

**Example 1.3:**
Evaluate $(a)$ $3 - 4[5 - 6(2 - 8)]$, $(b)$ $[3 - 8 \cdot 5 - (-1 - 2 \cdot 3)] \cdot (3^2 - 5^2)^2$.

$(a)$
$$3 - 4[5 - 6(2 - 8)] = 3 - 4[5 - 6(-6)]$$
$$= 3 - 4[5 + 36]$$
$$= 3 - 4[41] = 3 - 164 = -161$$

$(b)$
$$[3 - 8 \cdot 5 - (-1 - 2 \cdot 3)] \cdot (3^2 - 5^2)^2 = [3 - 8 \cdot 5 - (-1 - 6)] \cdot (9 - 25)^2$$
$$= [3 - (8 \cdot 5) - (-7)] \cdot (-16)^2$$
$$= [3 - 40 + 7] \cdot 256$$
$$= -30 \cdot 256 = -7,680$$

## Polynomials

A *polynomial* is an expression that can be written as a term or a sum of terms of the form $a x_1^{n_1} x_2^{n_2} \cdots x_m^{n_m}$, where the $a$ is a constant and the $x_1, \ldots,$ $x_m$ are variables. A polynomial of one term is called a *monomial*. A polynomial of two terms is called a *binomial*. A polynomial of three terms is called a *trinomial*.

**Example 1.4:** $5$, $-20$, $\pi$, $t$, $3x^2$, $-15x^3y^2$, $\frac{2}{3}xy^4zw$ are monomials.

**Example 1.5:** $x + 5$, $x^2 - y^2$, $3x^5y^7 - \sqrt{3}x^3z$ are binomials.

**Example 1.6:** $x + y + 4z$, $5x^2 - 3x+1$, $8xyz - 5x^2y + 20t^3u$ are trinomials.

The *degree* of a term in a polynomial is the exponent of the variable, or, if more than one variable is present, the sum of the exponents of the variables.

The degree of a polynomial with more than one term is the largest of the degrees of the individual terms.

**Example 1.7:** (*a*) $3x^8$ has degree 8; (*b*) $12xy^2z^2$ has degree 5; (*c*) $\pi$ has degree 0; (*d*) $x^4 + 3x^2 - 250$ has degree 4; (*e*) $x^3y^2 - 30x^4$ has degree 5.

Two or more terms are called *like terms* if they are both constants, or if they contain the same variables raised to the same exponents, and differ only, if at all, in their constant coefficients. Terms that are not like terms are called *unlike terms*.

**Example 1.8:** $3x$ and $5x$, $-16x^2y$ and $2x^2y$, $tu^5$ and $6tu^5$ are examples of like terms. 3 and $3x$, $a^3b^2$ and $a^2b^3$ are examples of unlike terms.

## Sums and Differences of Polynomials

The sum of two or more polynomials is found by combining like terms. The difference of two polynomials is found by using the definition of subtraction: $A - B = A + (-B)$.

**Example 1.9:**

$$
\begin{aligned}
(y^2 - 5y + 7) - (3y^2 - 5y + 12) &= (y^2 - 5y + 7) + (-3y^2 + 5y - 12) \\
&= y^2 - 5y + 7 - 3y^2 + 5y - 12 \\
&= -2y^2 - 5
\end{aligned}
$$

## Products of Polynomials

The product of two polynomials is found using the distributive property as well as the first law of exponents: $x^a x^b = x^{a+b}$

**Example 1.10:**

$$x^3(3x^4 - 5x^2 + 7x + 2) = x^3 \cdot 3x^4 - x^3 \cdot 5x^2 + x^3 \cdot 7x + x^3 \cdot 2$$
$$= 3x^7 - 5x^5 + 7x^4 + 2x^3$$

**Example 1.11:** Multiply $(x + 2y)(x^3 - 3x^2y + xy^2)$

$$(x + 2y)(x^3 - 3x^2y + xy^2) = (x + 2y)x^3 - (x + 2y)3x^2y + (x + 2y)xy^2$$
$$= x^4 + 2x^3y - 3x^3y - 6x^2y^2 + x^2y^2 + 2xy^3$$
$$= x^4 - x^3y - 5x^2y^2 + 2xy^3$$

Often a vertical format is used for this situation:

$$x^3 - 3x^2y + xy^2$$
$$x + 2y$$
$$\overline{x^4 - 3x^3y + x^2y^2}$$
$$2x^3y - 6x^2y^2 + 2xy^3$$
$$\overline{x^4 - x^3y - 5x^2y^2 + 2xy^3}$$

The FOIL (First Outer Inner Last) Method is frequently used for multiplying two binomials:

$$(a + b)(c + d) = ac + ad + bc + bd = \text{(First)} + \text{(Outer)} + \text{(Inner)} + \text{(Last)}$$

## Special Product Forms:

| | |
|---|---|
| $(a + b)(a - b) = a^2 - b^2$ | Difference of two squares |
| $(a + b)^2 = a^2 + 2ab + b^2$ | Square of a sum |
| $(a - b)^2 = a^2 - 2ab + b^2$ | Square of a difference |

# Factoring

Factoring polynomials reverses the distributive operations of multiplication. A polynomial that cannot be factored is called *prime*. Common factoring techniques include: removing a common factor; factoring by grouping; reverse FOIL factoring; and special factoring forms.

**Example 1.12:** A monomial factor:

$$3x^5 - 24x^4 + 12x^3 = 3x^3(x^2 - 8x + 4)$$

**Example 1.13:** A nonmonomial factor:

$$12(x^2-1)^4(3x+1)^3 + 8x(x^2-1)^3(3x+1)^4 = 4(x^2-1)^3(3x+1)^3[3(x^2-1)+2x(3x+1)]$$
$$= 4(x^2-1)^3(3x+1)^3(9x^2+2x-3)$$

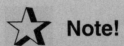 **Note!**

The common factor in such problems consists of each base to the lowest exponent present in each term.

**Example 1.14:** Factoring by grouping:

$$3x^2 + 4xy - 3xt - 4ty = (3x^2 + 4xy) - (3xt + 4ty)$$
$$= x(3x+4y) - t(3x+4y) = (3x+4y)(x-t)$$

Reverse FOIL factoring follows the patterns:

$$x^2 + (a+b)x + ab = (x+a)(x+b)$$
$$acx^2 + (bc+ad)xy + bdy^2 = (ax+by)(cx+dy)$$

**Example 1.15:** Reverse FOIL factoring:

(a) To factor $x^2 - 15x + 50$, find two factors of 50 that add to $-15$: $-5$ and $-10 \cdot x^2 - 15x + 50 = (x-5)(x-10)$

(b) To factor $4x^2 + 11xy + 6y^2$, find factors of $4 \cdot 6 = 24$ that add to 11: 8 and 3.
$$4x^2 + 11xy + 6y^2 = 4x^2 + 8xy + 3xy + 6y^2$$
$$= 4x(x+2y) + 3y(x+2y) = (x+2y)(4x+3y)$$

## General Factoring Strategy

*Step 1:*      Remove all factors common to all terms.
*Step 2:*      Note the number of terms. If the polynomial remaining after step 1 has:

(*a*) two terms, look for a difference of two squares, or a sum or difference of two cubes.

(*b*) three terms, look for a perfect square or try reverse FOIL factoring.

(*c*) four or more terms, try factoring by grouping.

## Special Factoring Forms

| | |
|---|---|
| $a^2 - b^2 = (a+b)(a-b)$ | Difference of two squares |
| $a^2 + b^2$ is prime. | Sum of two squares |
| $a^2 + 2ab + b^2 = (a+b)^2$ | Square of a sum |
| $a^2 - 2ab + b^2 = (a-b)^2$ | Square of a difference |

# Exponents

Natural number exponents are defined by $x^n = xx \ldots x$ ($n$ factors of $x$)

**Example 1.16:** $5a^3b + 3(2ab)^3 = 5aaab + 3(2ab)(2ab)(2ab)$

Note: $x^0 = 1$ for any nonzero real number $x$. $0^0$ is not defined. Negative integer exponents are defined by $x^{-n} = \dfrac{1}{x^n}$ for any nonzero real number $x$.

**Example 1.17:**

$$3x^{-2}y^4 + 2(3x)^{-4}y^{-5}z^2 = 3 \cdot \frac{1}{x^2}y^4 + 2 \cdot \frac{1}{(3x)^4} \cdot \frac{1}{y^5}z^2 = \frac{3y^4}{x^2} + \frac{2z^2}{(3x)^4 y^5}$$

Rational number exponents, $x^{1/n}$ (the principal $n$th root of $x$), are defined for $n$ an integer greater than 1 by:

• If $n$ is odd, $x^{1/n}$ is the unique real number $y$ which, when raised to the $n$th power, gives $x$.

• If $n$ is even, then,

– if $x > 0$, $x^{1/n}$ is the positive real number $y$ which, when raised to the $n$th power gives $x$.

- if $x = 0$, $x^{1/n} = 0$.
- if $x < 0$, $x^{1/n}$ is not a real number.

# Remember

Even roots of negative numbers are *not* real numbers.

**Example 1.18:** $(a)$ $16^{1/4} = 2$; $(b)$ $-16^{1/4} = -(16)^{1/4} = -2$; $(c)$ $(-16)^{1/4}$ is not a real number; $(d)$ $(-8)^{1/3} = -2$

$x^{m/n}$ is defined by: $x^{m/n} = (x^{1/n})^m = (x^m)^{1/n}$, provided $x^{1/n}$ is real.

$$x^{-m/n} = \frac{1}{x^{m/n}}$$

**Example 1.19:** $(a)$ $8^{-4/3} = \dfrac{1}{8^{4/3}} = \dfrac{1}{(8^{1/3})^4} = \dfrac{1}{2^4} = \dfrac{1}{16}$, $(b)$ $(-64)^{5/6}$ is not a real number.

Laws of exponents for $a$ and $b$ rational numbers and $x$ and $y$ real numbers (avoiding even roots of negative numbers and division by 0):

$$x^a x^b = x^{a+b} \quad (xy)^a = x^a y^a \quad (x^a)^b = x^{ab} \quad \left(\frac{x}{y}\right)^a = \frac{x^a}{y^a}$$

$$\frac{x^a}{x^b} = x^{b-a} \quad \frac{x^a}{x^b} = \frac{1}{x^{b-a}} \quad \left(\frac{x}{y}\right)^{-m} = \left(\frac{y}{x}\right)^m \quad \frac{x^{-n}}{y^{-m}} = \frac{y^m}{x^n}$$

# Rational and Radical Expressions

A *rational expression* is one which can be written as the quotient of two polynomials. Rational expressions are defined for all real values of the variables except those that make the denominator equal to zero.

Recall that one of the Laws of Quotients is:

$\dfrac{a}{b} = \dfrac{ak}{bk}$ (building to higher terms) or $\dfrac{ak}{bk} = \dfrac{a}{b}$ (reducing to lower terms)

**Example 1.20:** Reducing to lowest terms:

$$\frac{x^2 - 2xy + y^2}{x^2 - y^2} = \frac{(x-y)^2}{(x-y)(x+y)} = \frac{x-y}{x+y}$$

## Operations on Rational Expressions

$$\left(\frac{a}{b}\right)^{-1} = \frac{b}{a} \qquad \frac{a}{b} \cdot \frac{c}{d} = \frac{ac}{bd} \qquad \frac{a}{b} \div \frac{c}{d} = \frac{a}{b} \cdot \left(\frac{c}{d}\right)^{-1} = \frac{a}{b} \cdot \frac{d}{c} = \frac{ad}{bc}$$

$$\frac{a}{c} \pm \frac{b}{c} = \frac{a \pm b}{c} \qquad \frac{a}{b} \pm \frac{c}{d} = \frac{ad}{bd} \pm \frac{bc}{bd} = \frac{ad \pm bc}{bd}$$

*Complex fractions* are expressions containing fractions in the numerator and/or denominator. They can be reduced to simple fractions by two methods:

*Method 1:* Combine numerator and denominator into single quotients, then divide.

**Example 1.21:**

$$\frac{\dfrac{x}{x-1} - \dfrac{a}{a-1}}{x-a} = \frac{\dfrac{x(a-1) - a(x-1)}{(x-1)(a-1)}}{x-a} = \frac{xa - x - ax + a}{(x-1)(a-1)} \div (x-a)$$

$$= \frac{a-x}{(x-1)(a-1)} \cdot \frac{1}{x-a} = \frac{-1}{(x-1)(a-1)}$$

*Method 2:* Multiply numerator and denominator by the lowest common denominator (LCD) of all internal fractions.

**Example 1.22:**

$$\frac{\dfrac{x}{y} - \dfrac{y}{x}}{\dfrac{x}{y^2} + \dfrac{y}{x^2}} = \frac{\dfrac{x}{y} - \dfrac{y}{x}}{\dfrac{x}{y^2} + \dfrac{y}{x^2}} \cdot \frac{x^2 y^2}{x^2 y^2} = \frac{x^3 y - xy^3}{x^3 + y^3} = \frac{xy(x-y)(x+y)}{(x+y)(x^2 - xy + y^2)} = \frac{xy(x-y)}{x^2 - xy + y^2}$$

Rational expressions are often written in terms of negative exponents.

**Example 1.23:** Simplify $x^{-3}y^5 - 3x^{-4}y^6$.

This can be done in two ways:

(a) $x^{-4}y^5(x - 3y) = \dfrac{y^5(x - 3y)}{x^4}$

(b) $\dfrac{y^5}{x^3} - \dfrac{3y^6}{x^4} = \dfrac{xy^5}{x^4} - \dfrac{3y^6}{x^4} = \dfrac{xy^5 - 3y^6}{x^4} = \dfrac{y^5(x - 3)}{x^4}$

## Radical Expressions

For a natural number $n$ greater than 1 and a real number $x$, the *nth root radical* is defined to be the principal $n$th root of $x$: $\sqrt[n]{x} = x^{1/n}$

### Note!

The *square root* of $x$ is written
$\sqrt{x}$ instead of $\sqrt[2]{x}$.

The symbol $\sqrt{\phantom{x}}$ is called a radical, $n$ is called the index, and $x$ is called the radicand.

## Conversion of Radical Expression to Exponent Form

For $m$, $n$ positive integers ($n > 1$) and $x \geq 0$ when $n$ is even,

$$x^{m/n} = \sqrt[n]{x^m} = \left(\sqrt[n]{x}\right)^m.$$

## Simplification of Radicals

In general, each of the following conditions indicates simplification of the radical expression is possible:
1. The radicand contains a factor with an exponent greater than or equal to the index of the radical.
2. The radicand and the index of the radical have a common factor other than 1.

3. A radical appears in a denominator.
4. A fraction appears in a radical.

**Example 1.24:**

(*a*) Condition 1:

$$\sqrt[3]{16x^3y^5} = \sqrt[3]{8x^3y^3 \cdot 2y^2} = \sqrt[3]{8x^3y^3} \cdot \sqrt[3]{2y^2} = 2xy\sqrt[3]{2y^2}$$

(*b*) Condition 2: $\sqrt[6]{t^3} = \sqrt[2\cdot3]{t^3} = \sqrt{\sqrt[3]{t^3}} = \sqrt{t}$

(*c*) Condition 3 (*rationalizing the denominator*):

$$\frac{12x^2}{\sqrt[4]{27xy^2}} = \frac{12x^2}{\sqrt[4]{27xy^2}} \cdot \frac{\sqrt[4]{3x^3y^2}}{\sqrt[4]{3x^3y^2}} = \frac{12x^2\sqrt[4]{3x^3y^2}}{\sqrt[4]{81x^4y^4}} = \frac{12x^2\sqrt[4]{3x^3y^2}}{3xy} = \frac{4x\sqrt[4]{3x^3y^2}}{y}$$

(*d*) Condition 4: $\sqrt[4]{\dfrac{3x}{5y^3}} = \sqrt[4]{\dfrac{3x}{5y^3} \cdot \dfrac{5^3y}{5^3y}} = \sqrt[4]{\dfrac{375xy}{5^4y^4}} = \dfrac{\sqrt[4]{375xy}}{5y}$

The *conjugate* expression for a binomial of form $a + b$ is the expression $a - b$ and conversely.

To rationalize the denominator of an expression, multiply the numerator and denominator by the conjugate of the denominator.

To rationalize the numerator, multiply the numerator and denominator by the conjugate of the numerator.

**Example 1.25:** Rationalize the denominator of $\dfrac{x-4}{\sqrt{x}-2}$.

$$\frac{x-4}{\sqrt{x}-2} = \frac{x-4}{\sqrt{x}-2} \cdot \frac{\sqrt{x}+2}{\sqrt{x}+2} = \frac{(x-4)(\sqrt{x}+2)}{x-4} = \sqrt{x}+2$$

**Example 1.26:** Rationalize the numerator of $\dfrac{\sqrt{x}-\sqrt{a}}{x-a}$.

$$\frac{\sqrt{x}-\sqrt{a}}{x-a} = \frac{\sqrt{x}-\sqrt{a}}{x-a} \cdot \frac{\sqrt{x}+\sqrt{a}}{\sqrt{x}+\sqrt{a}} = \frac{x-a}{(x-a)(\sqrt{x}+\sqrt{a})} = \frac{1}{\sqrt{x}+\sqrt{a}}$$

# Chapter 2
# EQUATIONS AND INEQUALITIES

IN THIS CHAPTER:

✔ *Equations*
✔ *Linear Equations*
✔ *Quadratic Equations*
✔ *Radical Equations*
✔ *Applications*
✔ *Inequalities*
✔ *Absolute Value in Equations
and Inequalities*
✔ *Parametric Equations*

## Equations

An *equation* is a statement that two expressions are equal. An equation containing variables is in general neither true nor false; rather, its truth depends on the value(s) of the variable(s). For equations in one variable, a value of the variable that makes the equation true is called a *solution* of the equation. The set of all solutions is called the *solution set* of the equation. An equation that is true for all those values of the variable for which it is meaningful is called an *identity*.

Equations are *equivalent* if they have the same solution sets.

**Example 2.1:** The equations $x = -5$ and $x + 5 = 0$ are equivalent. Each has the solution set $\{-5\}$.

**Example 2.2:** The equations $x^2 = 25$ and $x = 5$ are not equivalent. The first has the solution set $\{-5, 5\}$, while the second equation has the solution set $\{5\}$.

The process of solving an equation consists of transforming it into an equivalent equation whose solution is obvious. Operations of transforming an equation into an equivalent equation include the following:

1.  Adding the same number to both sides. Thus, the equations $a = b$ and $a + c = b + c$ are equivalent.
2.  Subtracting the same number from both sides. Thus, the equations $a = b$ and $a - c = b - c$ are equivalent.
3.  Multiplying both sides by the same nonzero number. Thus, the equations $a = b$ and $ac = bc$, $(c \neq 0)$ are equivalent.
4.  Dividing both sides by the same nonzero number. Thus, the equations $a = b$ and $\dfrac{a}{c} = \dfrac{b}{c}$, $(c \neq 0)$ are equivalent.
5.  Simplifying expressions on either side of an equation.

# Linear Equations

A *linear equation* is one that is in the form $ax + b = 0$ or can be transformed into an equivalent equation in this form. If $a \neq 0$, a linear equation has exactly one solution. If $a = 0$ the equation has no solutions unless $b = 0$, in which case the equation is an identity. An equation that is not linear is called *nonlinear*.

**Example 2.3:** $2x + 6 = 0$ is an example of a linear equation in one variable. It has one solution, $-3$. Therefore, the solution set is $\{-3\}$.

**Example 2.4:** $x^2 = 16$ is an example of a nonlinear equation in one variable. It has two solutions, 4 and $-4$. The solution set is $\{4, -4\}$.

Linear equations are solved by the process of isolating the variable. The equation is transformed into equivalent equations by simplification, combining all variable terms on one side, all constant terms on the other, then dividing both sides by the coefficient of the variable.

**Example 2.5:** Solve the equation $3x - 8 = 7x + 9$.

$$3x - 8 = 7x + 9 \quad \text{Subtract } 7x \text{ from both sides.}$$
$$-4x - 8 = 9 \quad \text{Add 8 to both sides.}$$
$$-4x = 17 \quad \text{Divide both sides by } -4.$$
$$x = -\frac{17}{4} \quad \text{Solution set is } \left\{ -\frac{17}{4} \right\}$$

# Quadratic Equations

A *quadratic equation* is one that is in the form $ax^2 + bx + c = 0$, $(a \neq 0)$ (*standard form*), or that can be transformed into this form. There are four methods for solving quadratic equations.

1. **Factoring.** If the polynomial $ax^2 + bx + c$ has linear factors with rational coefficients, write it in factored form, then apply the zero-factor property that $AB = 0$ only if $A = 0$ or $B = 0$.
2. **Square Root Property.** If the equation is in the form $A^2 = b$, where $b$ is a constant, then its solutions are found as $A = \sqrt{b}$ and $A = -\sqrt{b}$, generally written $A = \pm\sqrt{b}$.
3. **Completing the Square.**
   (a) Write the equation in the form $x^2 + px = q$
   (b) Add $p^2/4$ to both sides to form $x^2 + px + p^2/4 = q + p^2/4$.
   (c) The left side is now a perfect square. Write
       $(x + p/2)^2 = q + p^2/4$ and apply the square root property.
4. **Quadratic Formula.** The solutions of $ax^2 + bx + c = 0$, $(a \neq 0)$ can always be written as:

$$x = \frac{-b \pm \sqrt{b^2 - 4ac}}{2a}$$

In general, a quadratic equation is solved by first checking whether it is easily factorable. If it is, then the factoring method is used; otherwise the quadratic formula is used.

**Example 2.6:** (factoring) Solve $3x^2 + 5x + 2 = 0$.

$$3x^2 + 5x + 2 = 0 \quad \text{Polynomial is factorable using integers}$$
$$(3x + 2)(x + 1) = 0 \quad \text{Apply the zero-factor property}$$
$$3x + 2 = 0 \quad \text{or} \quad x + 1 = 0$$
$$x = -2/3 \quad \text{or} \quad x = -1$$

**Example 2.7:** (complete the square) Solve $2x^2 - 3x + 6 = 0$.

$$2x^2 - 3x + 6 = 0 \qquad \text{Polynomial is not factorable}$$

$$x^2 - \frac{3}{2}x = -3 \qquad \text{Write in the form } x^2 + px = q$$

$$x^2 - \frac{3}{2}x + \frac{9}{16} = -3 + \frac{9}{16} \qquad \text{Add } p^2/4 \text{ to both sides}$$

$$\left(x - \frac{3}{4}\right)^2 = -\frac{39}{16} \qquad \text{Write } (x + p/2)^2 = q + p^2/4$$

$$x - \frac{3}{4} = \pm\sqrt{\frac{-39}{16}} \qquad \text{Apply the square root property}$$

$$x = \frac{3 \pm \sqrt{39}i}{4}$$

**Example 2.8:** (quadratic formula) Solve $x^2 + 5x + 2 = 0$.

$$x^2 + 5x + 2 = 0 \qquad \text{Polynomial is not factorable}$$

$$x = \frac{-5 \pm \sqrt{25 - 4 \cdot 1 \cdot 2}}{2 \cdot 1} \qquad a = 1, b = 5, c = 2$$

$$x = \frac{-5 \pm \sqrt{17}}{2}$$

In the quadratic formula, the quantity $b^2 - 4ac$ is called the *discriminant*. The sign of this quantity determines the number and type of solutions of a quadratic equation:

| Sign of discriminant | Number and type of solutions |
| :---: | :---: |
| positive | 2 real solutions |
| zero | 1 repeated real solution |
| negative | 2 imaginary solutions |

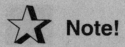 **Note!**

Many equations that are not at first glace linear or quadratic can be reduced to linear or quadratic equations, or can be solved by a factoring method.

**Example 2.9:** Solve $x^3 - 5x^2 - 4x + 20 = 0$.

$$x^3 - 5x^2 - 4x + 20 = 0 \quad \text{Factor by grouping}$$
$$x^2(x - 5) - 4(x - 5) = 0$$
$$(x - 5)(x^2 - 4) = 0$$
$$(x - 5)(x + 2)(x - 2) = 0$$
$$x = 5 \text{ or } x = -2 \text{ or } x = 2$$

**Example 2.10:** Solve $\dfrac{6}{x+1} = 5 - \dfrac{6x}{x+1}$.

Multiply both sides by $x + 1$, the only denominator. Note: $x \neq -1$.

$$\frac{6}{x+1} = 5 - \frac{6x}{x+1}$$
$$(x+1) \cdot \frac{6}{x+1} = 5(x+1) - \frac{6x}{x+1} \cdot (x+1)$$
$$6 = 5x + 5 - 6x$$
$$1 = -x$$
$$x = -1$$

In this case, since $x \neq -1$, there can be no solution.

## Radical Equations

Equations containing radicals require an additional operation: In general, the equation $a = b$ is not equivalent to the equation $a^n = b^n$; however, if $n$ is odd, they have the same real solutions. If $n$ is even, all solutions of $a = b$ are found among the solutions of $a^n = b^n$. Hence it is permissible to raise both sides to an even power if all solutions of the resulting equation are checked to see if they are solutions of the original equation.

**Example 2.11:** Solve $\sqrt{x+2} = x - 4$.

$$\left(\sqrt{x+2}\right)^2 = (x-4)^2$$
$$x + 2 = x^2 - 8x + 16$$
$$0 = x^2 - 9x + 14$$
$$0 = (x-7)(x-2)$$
$$x = 2 \text{ or } x = 7$$

Check: $x = 2: \sqrt{2+2} = 2-4$?    $x = 7: \sqrt{7+2} = 7-4$?

$2 \neq -2$ $3 = 3$

Not a solution 7 is the only solution

# Applications

In formulas, literal equations, and equations in more than one variable, letters are used as coefficients rather than particular numbers. However, the procedures for solving for a specified variable are essentially the same; the other variables are simply treated as constants.

**Example 2.12:** Solve $A = P + Prt$ for $P$.

This equation is linear in $P$, the specified variable. Factor out $P$, then divide by the coefficient of $P$.

$$A = P + Prt$$

$$A = P(1 + rt)$$

$$\frac{A}{1 + rt} = P$$

$$P = \frac{A}{1 + rt}$$

**Example 2.13:** Solve $s = \frac{1}{2}gt^2$ for $t$.

This equation is quadratic in $t$, the specified variable. Isolate $t^2$, then apply the square root property.

$$s = \frac{1}{2}gt^2$$

$$\frac{2s}{g} = t^2$$

$$t = \pm\sqrt{\frac{2s}{g}}$$

Frequently, but not always, in applied situations, only the positive solutions are retained: $t = \sqrt{2s/g}$.

In application problems a situation is described and questions are posed in ordinary language. It is necessary to form a model of the situa-

tion using variables to stand for unknown quantities, construct an equation (or inequality or system of equations) that describes the relation
among the quantities, solve the equation, then interpret the solution to answer the original questions.

**Example 2.14:** A right triangle has sides whose lengths are three con-
secutive even integers. Find the lengths of the sides.
Sketch a figure as in Figure 2-1:

$$
\begin{array}{ll}
\text{Let} & x = \text{length of shortest side} \\
& x + 2 = \text{length of next side} \\
& x + 4 = \text{length of hypotenuse}
\end{array}
$$

(triangle with sides labeled $x + 4$, $x$, and $x + 2$)

**Figure 2-1**

Now apply the Pythagorean theorem: In a right triangle with sides $a$, $b$,
$c$, $a^2 + b^2 = c^2$. Hence,

$$x^2 + (x+2)^2 = (x+4)^2$$
$$x^2 + x^2 + 4x + 4 = x^2 + 8x + 16$$
$$2x^2 + 4x + 4 = x^2 + 8x + 16$$
$$x^2 - 4x - 12 = 0$$
$$(x-6)(x+2) = 0$$

$$x = 6 \text{ or } x = -2$$

The negative answer is discarded. Hence, the lengths of the sides are: $x$
$= 6$, $x + 2 = 8$, and $x + 4 = 10$.

## Variation

The term *variation* is used to describe many
forms of simple dependence. The general pattern
is that one variable, called the *dependent variable*, is said to vary as a result of changes in one
or more other variables, called the *independent
variables*. Variation statements always include a
nonzero constant multiple, referred to as the constant of variation, or constant of proportionality,
and often denoted $k$.

*Direct variation* is a relation of the form $y = kx$. The following language is used to describe this type of relation:

1. $y$ varies directly as $x$ (occasionally, $y$ varies as $x$).
2. $y$ is directly proportional to $x$.

**Example 2.15:** Given that $p$ varies directly as $q$, find an expression for $p$ in terms of $q$ if $p = 300$ when $q = 12$.

Since $p$ varies directly as $q$, write $p = kq$. Since $p = 300$ when $q = 12$, substitute these values to obtain $300 = k(12)$, or $k = 25$. Hence $p = 25q$.

*Inverse variation* is a relation of the form $xy = k$, or $y = k/x$. The following language is used to describe a relation of this form:

1. $y$ varies inversely as $x$.
2. $y$ is inversely proportional to $x$.

**Example 2.16:** Given that $s$ varies inversely as $t$, find an expression for $s$ in terms of $t$ if $s = 5$ when $t = 8$.

Since $s$ varies inversely as $t$, write $s = k/t$. Since $s = 5$ when $t = 8$, substitute these values to obtain $5 = k/8$, or $k = 40$. Hence $s = 40/t$.

*Joint variation* describes a relation of the form $z = kxy$. The following language is used to describe a relation of this form:

1. $z$ varies jointly as $x$ and $y$.
2. $z$ varies directly as the product of $x$ and $y$.

**Example 2.17:** Given that $z$ varies jointly as $x$ and $y$ and $z = 3$ when $x = 4$ and $y = 5$, find an expression for $z$ in terms of $x$ and $y$.

Since $z$ varies jointly as $x$ and $y$, write $z = kxy$. Since $z = 3$ when $x = 4$ and $y = 5$, substitute these values to obtain $3 = k \cdot 4 \cdot 5$, or $k = \dfrac{3}{20}$. Hence $z = \dfrac{3}{20} xy$.

**Example 2.18:** If $P$ varies jointly as the fourth root of $y$ and the square of $x$, and $P = 24$ when $x = 12$ and $y = 81$, find $P$ when $x = 1200$ and $y = \dfrac{1}{16}$.

Since $P$ varies jointly as the fourth root of $y$ and the square of $x$, write $P = k\sqrt[4]{y}x^2$. Since $P = 24$ when $x = 12$ and $y = 81$, substitute these values to obtain $24 = k\sqrt[4]{81}(12)^2$ or $k = \dfrac{1}{18}$. Hence $P = \dfrac{\sqrt[4]{y}x^2}{18}$. Thus when

$x = 1200$ and $y = \dfrac{1}{16}$, $P = \dfrac{\sqrt[4]{1/16}(1200)^2}{18} = 40,000$.

## Inequalities

If $a < x$ and $x < b$, the two statements are often combined to write $a < x < b$. The set of all real numbers $x$ satisfying $a < x < b$ is called an open interval and is written $(a, b)$. Similarly the set of all real numbers $x$ satisfying the combined inequality $a \le x \le b$ is called a closed interval and is written $[a, b]$. The following table shows various common inequalities and their interval representations.

| Inequality | Notation | Graph |
|---|---|---|
| $a < x < b$ | $(a, b)$ | |
| $a \le x \le b$ | $[a, b]$ | |
| $a < x \le b$ | $(a, b]$ | |
| $a \le x < b$ | $[a, b)$ | |

| Inequality | Notation | Graph |
|---|---|---|
| $x > a$ | $(a, \infty)$ | |
| $x \ge a$ | $[a, \infty)$ | |
| $x < b$ | $(-\infty, b)$ | |
| $x \le b$ | $(-\infty, b]$ | |

An inequality statement involving variables, like an equation, is in general neither true nor false; rather, its truth depends on the value(s) of the variable(s). For inequality statements in one variable, a value of the variable that makes the statement true is a solution to the inequality. The set of all solutions is called the *solution set* of the inequality.

## Remember

Inequalities are equivalent if they have the same solution sets.

**Example 2.19:** The inequalities $x < -5$ and $x + 5 < 0$ are equivalent. Each has the solution set consisting of all real numbers less than $-5$, that is, $(-\infty, -5)$.

The process of solving an inequality consists of transforming it into an equivalent inequality whose solution is obvious. Operations of transforming an inequality into equivalent inequality include the following:

1. Adding or subtracting: The inequalities $a < b$, $a + c < b + c$, and $a - c < b - c$ are equivalent for $c$ any real number.
2. Multiplying and dividing by a positive number: The inequalities $a < b$, $ac < ab$, and $a/c < b/c$ are equivalent for $c$ any positive real number.
3. Multiplying and dividing by a negative number: The inequalities $a < b$, $ac > ab$, and $a/c > b/c$ are equivalent for $c$ any negative real number. Note that the sense of an inequality reverses upon multiplication or division by a negative number.
4. Simplifying expressions on either side of an inequality.

## Linear Inequalities

A *linear inequality* is one which is in the form $ax + b < 0$, $ax + b > 0$, $ax + b \leq 0$, or $ax + b \geq 0$, or can be transformed into an equivalent inequality in this form. In general, linear inequalities have infinite solutions sets in one of the forms shown in the table above. Linear inequalities are solved by isolating the variable in a manner similar to solving equations.

**Example 2.20:** Solve $5 - 3x > 4$.

$$5 - 3x > 4$$
$$- 3x > - 1$$
$$x < 1/3$$

Note that the sense of the inequality was reversed by dividing both sides by $- 3$.

## Nonlinear Inequalities

An inequality for which the left side can be written as a product or quotient of linear factors (or prime quadratic factors) can be solved through a sign diagram. If any such factor is not zero on an interval, then it is either positive on the whole interval or negative on the whole interval. Hence:

1.  Determine the points at which each factor is 0. These are called the *critical points.*
2.  Draw a number line and show the critical points.
3.  Determine the sign of each factor in each interval; then, using laws of multiplication or division, determine the sign of the entire quantity on the left side of the inequality.
4.  Write the solution set.

**Example 2.21:** Solve $(x - 1)(x + 2) > 0$.

The critical points are 1 and − 2, where, respectively, $x - 1$ and $x + 2$ are zero. Draw a number line showing the critical points (see Figure 2-2). These points divide the real number line into the intervals $(- \infty, - 2)$, $(- 2, 1)$, and $(1, \infty)$. In $(- \infty, - 2)$, $x - 1$ and $x + 2$ are negative; hence the product is positive. In $(- 2, 1)$, $x - 1$ is negative and $x + 2$ is positive; hence, the product is negative. In $(1, \infty)$, both factors are positive; hence the product is positive.

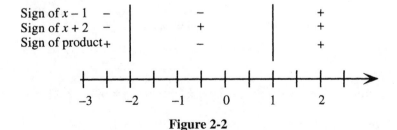

**Figure 2-2**

The inequality holds when $(x - 1)(x + 2)$ is positive. Hence the solution set consists of the intervals: $(-\infty, -2) \cup (1, \infty)$.

## Absolute Value in Equations and Inequalities

### Remember

$$|a| = \begin{cases} a & \text{if } a \geq 0 \\ -a & \text{if } a < 0 \end{cases}$$

Geometrically, the absolute value of a real number is the distance of that number from the origin (see Figure 2-3).

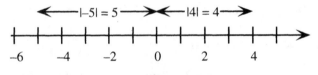

$$\longleftarrow |-5| = 5 \longrightarrow \longleftarrow |4| = 4 \longrightarrow$$

$$-6 \qquad -4 \qquad -2 \qquad 0 \qquad 2 \qquad 4$$

**Figure 2-3**

Similarly, the distance between two real numbers $a$ and $b$ is the absolute value of their difference: $|a - b|$ or $|b - a|$.

### Properties of Absolute Values

$$|-a| = |a| \qquad |a| = \sqrt{a^2}$$
$$|ab| = |a||b| \qquad |a + b| \leq |a| + |b|$$

**Example 2.22:** $(a)\ |-5x^2| = |-5||x^2| = 5x^2;\ (b)\ |3y| = |3||y| = 3|y|$

**Example 2.23:** $|5 + (-7)| = 2 \leq |5| + |-7| = 5 + 7 = 12$

## Absolute Value in Equations

Since $|a|$ is the distance of $a$ from the origin,

1.  The equation $|a| = b$ is equivalent to the two equations $a = b$ and $a = -b$, for $b > 0$. (The distance of $a$ from the origin will equal $b$ precisely when $a$ equals $b$ or $-b$.)
2.  The equation $|a| = |b|$ is equivalent to the two equations $a = b$ and $a = -b$.

Therefore, to solve an equation containing absolute values, transform it into equivalent equations that do not contain the absolute value symbol and solve.

**Example 2.24:** Solve $|x + 3| = 5$.

$$x + 3 = 5 \quad \text{or} \quad x + 3 = -5$$
$$x = 2 \qquad\qquad x = -8$$

**Example 2.25:** Solve $|x - 4| = |3x + 1|$.

$$x - 4 = 3x + 1 \quad \text{or} \quad x - 4 = -(3x + 1)$$
$$-2x = 5 \qquad\qquad x - 4 = -3x - 1$$
$$x = -\frac{5}{2} \qquad\qquad x = \frac{3}{4}$$

## Absolute Value in Inequalities

1.  For $b > 0$, the inequality $|a| < b$ is equivalent to the double inequality $-b < a < b$. (Since the distance of $a$ from the origin is *less* than $b$, $a$ is closer to the origin than $b$; see Figure 2-4.)

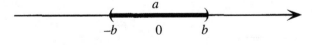

**Figure 2-4**

2.  For $b > 0$, the inequality $|a| > b$ is equivalent to the inequalities $a > b$ and $a < -b$. (Since the distance of $a$ from the origin is greater than $b$, $a$ is further from the origin than $b$; see Figure 2-5.)

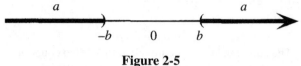

**Figure 2-5**

**Example 2.26:** $|x - 5| > 3$

$$x - 5 > 3 \quad \text{or} \quad x - 5 < -3$$
$$x > 8 \qquad\qquad\qquad x < 2$$

# Parametric Equations

An equation for a curve may be given by specifying $x$ and $y$ separately as functions of a third variable, often $t$, called a parameter. These functions are called the *parametric equations* for the curve. Points on the curve may be found by assigning permissible values of $t$. Often, $t$ may be eliminated algebraically, but any restrictions placed on $t$ are needed to determine the portion of the curve that is specified by the parametric equations.

**Example 2.27:** Graph the curve specified by the parametric equations $x = 1 - t, y = 2t + 2$.

First note that $t$ can be eliminated by solving the equation specifying $x$ for $t$ to obtain $t = 1 - x$, then substituting into the equation specifying $y$ to obtain $y = 2(1 - x) + 2 = 4 - 2x$. Thus for every value of $t$, the point $(x,y)$ lies on the graph of $y = 4 - 2x$. Moreover, since there are no restrictions on $t$, it follows that $x$ and $y$ can take on any value. Form a table of values, then plot the points and connect them (Figure 2-6).

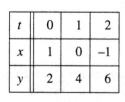

| $t$ | 0 | 1 | 2 |
|-----|---|---|----|
| $x$ | 1 | 0 | -1 |
| $y$ | 2 | 4 | 6 |

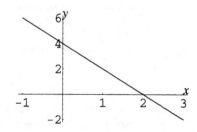

**Figure 2-6**

# Chapter 3
# SYSTEMS OF EQUATIONS AND PARTIAL FRACTIONS

IN THIS CHAPTER:

- ✔ *Systems of Equations*
- ✔ *Solving Linear Systems in Two Variables*
- ✔ *Solving Linear Systems in More than Two Variables*
- ✔ *Partial Fraction Decomposition*
- ✔ *Nonlinear Systems of Equations*

## Systems of Equations

A *system of equations* consists of two or more equations, considered as simultaneous specifications on more than one variable. A *solution* to a system of equations is an ordered assignment of values of the variables that, when substituted, would make each of the equations into true statements. The process of finding the solutions of a system is called *solving* the system. The set of all solutions is called the *solution set* of the system. Systems with the same solution set are called *equivalent* systems.

**Example 3.1:** Verify that $(x, y) = (-4, 2)$ is a solution to the system

$$y^2 + x = 0 \quad (1)$$

$$2x + 3y = -2 \quad (2)$$

If $x = -4$ and $y = 2$, then equation (1) becomes $2^2 + (-4) = 0$ and equation (2) becomes $2(-4) + 3 \cdot 2 = -2$. Since these are both true statements, $(x, y) = (-4, 2)$ is a solution to the system.

A linear equation in several variables is one that can be written in the form $a_1 x_1 + a_2 x_2 + \ldots + a_n x_n = b$, where $a_i$ are constants. This is referred to as *standard form*. If all equations of a system are linear, the system is called a *linear system*.

Equivalent systems of linear equations can be produced by the following operations on equations.

1.  Interchanging two equations.
2.  Replacing an equation by a nonzero multiple of itself.
3.  Replacing an equation by the result of adding the equation to a multiple of another equation.

## You Need to Know

It is understood that "adding two equations" means adding left side to left side and right side to right side to produce a new equation and "multiple of an equation" means the result of multiplying left side and right side by the same constant.

Systems of linear equations fall into one of three categories:

1.  *Consistent and independent.* Such systems have exactly one solution.
2.  *Inconsistent.* Such systems have no solutions.
3.  *Dependent.* Such systems have an infinite number of solutions.

# Solving Linear Systems in Two Variables

Solutions of linear systems in two variables are found by three methods:

1.  **Graphical Method.** Graph each equation (each graph is a straight line). If the lines intersect in a single point, the coordinates of this point may be read from the graph. After checking by substitution in each equation, these coordinates are the solution of the system. If the lines coincide, the system is dependent, and there are an infinite  number of solutions, with each solution of one equation being a solution of the others. If neither of these situations occurs, the system is inconsistent.

2.  **Substitution Method.** Solve one equation for one variable in terms of the other. Substitute this expression into the other equations to determine the value of the first variable (if possible). Then substitute this value to determine the value of the other variable.

3.  **Elimination Method.** Apply the operations on equations leading to equivalent systems to eliminate one variable from one equation, solve the resulting equation for this variable, and substitute this value to determine the value of the other variable.

In methods 2 and 3, the occurrence of an equation of the form $a = b$, where $a$ and $b$ are unequal constants, indicates an inconsistent system. If this does not occur, but all equations except one reduce to $0 = 0$, the system is dependent, and there are an infinite number of solutions, with each solution of one equation being a solution of the others.

**Example 3.2:** Solve the system
$$2x + 3y = 6 \quad (1)$$
$$-3x - y = 5 \quad (2)$$

(*a*) graphically, (*b*) by substitution, and (*c*) by elimination.

    (*a*) Graph the two equations (Figure 3-1):

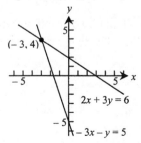

$(-3, 4)$

$2x + 3y = 6$

$-3x - y = 5$

**Figure 3-1**

The two lines appear to intersect at (−3, 4). It is necessary to check this result: substituting $x = -3$ and $y = 4$ into equations (1) and (2) yields

$$2(-3) + 3 \cdot 4 = 6 \qquad\qquad -3(-3) - 4 = 5$$

and

$$6 = 6 \qquad\qquad 5 = 5$$

respectively. Thus (−3, 4) is the only solution of the system.

    *(b)* It is correct to begin by solving either equation for either variable in terms of the other. The simplest choice seems to be to solve equation (2) for $y$ in terms of $x$ to obtain:

$$y = -3x - 5$$

Substitute the expression $-3x - 5$ for $y$ in equation (1) to obtain:

$$2x + 3(-3x - 5) = 6$$
$$-7x - 15 = 6$$
$$-7x = 21$$
$$x = -3$$

Substitute −3 for $x$ in equation (2) to obtain:

$$-3(-3) - y = 5$$
$$9 - y = 5$$
$$y = 4$$

Again, (−3, 4) is the only solution of the system.

    *(c)* If equation (2) is multiplied by 3, the coefficient of $y$ will "match" the coefficient of $y$ in equation (1); that is, it will be equal in absolute value and opposite in sign. Equation (2) then becomes

$$-9x - 3y = 15 \quad (3)$$

If equation (1) is replaced by itself plus this multiple of equation (2), the following equivalent system results:

$$-7x = 21 \quad (4)$$
$$-3x - y = 5 \quad (2)$$

From equation (4), $x = -3$. Substituting into equation (2) yields $y = 4$, as before.

# Solving Linear Systems in More than Two Variables

Solutions of linear systems in more than two variables are found by two methods:

1. **Substitution Method.** Solve one equation for one variable in terms of the others. Substitute this expression into the other equations to obtain a system with one fewer variable. If this process can be continued until an equation in one variable is obtained, solve the resulting equation for this variable, and substitute this value to determine the value of the other variables.

2. **Elimination Method.** Apply the operations on equations leading to equivalent systems to eliminate one variable from all equations except one. This leads to a system with one fewer variable. If this process can be continued until an equation in one variable is obtained, solve the resulting equation for this variable, and substitute this value to determine the value of the other variables.

Again, the occurrence of an equation of the form $a = b$, where $a$ and $b$ are unequal constants, indicates an inconsistent system. If this does not occur, but one or more equations reduce to $0 = 0$, leaving fewer nontrivial equations than there are variables, the system is dependent, and there are an infinite number of solutions, with each solution of one equation being a solution of the others.

**Example 3.3:** Solve the system

$$x - 3y + 2z = 14 \quad (1)$$
$$2x + 5y - z = -9 \quad (2)$$
$$-3x - y + 2z = 2 \quad (3)$$

*(a)* by substitution and *(b)* by elimination.

(a) Solve equation (1) for $x$ to obtain

$$x = 3y - 2z + 14 \quad (4)$$

Substitute the expression $3y - 2z + 14$ for $x$ from equation (4) into equations (2) and (3).

$$2(3y - 2z + 14) + 5y - z = -9$$
$$-3(3y - 2z + 14) - y + 2z = 2$$

Simplifying yields:

$$11y - 5z = -37 \quad (5)$$
$$-10y + 8z = 44 \quad (6)$$

Solve equation (5) for $y$ to obtain

$$y = \frac{5z - 37}{11} \quad (7)$$

Substitute the expression on the right for $y$ into equation (6).

$$-10\left(\frac{5z - 37}{11}\right) + 8z = 44$$

$$-50z + 370 + 88z = 484$$

$$38z = 114$$

$$z = 3$$

Substituting this value for $z$ into equation (7) yields $y = -2$. Substituting $y = -2$ and $z = 3$ into equation (4) yields $x = 2$. The solution is written as the *ordered triple* $(2, -2, 3)$.

*(b)* Replacing equation (2) by itself plus $-2$ times equation (1) will eliminate $x$ from equation (2). Thus:

$$2x + 5y - z = -9 \qquad\qquad\qquad (2)$$
$$\underline{-2x + 6y - 4z = -28} \qquad\qquad (-2) \cdot \text{Eq. (1)}$$
$$11y - 5z = -37 \qquad\qquad\qquad (5)$$

Similarly, replacing equation (3) by itself plus 3 times equation (1) will eliminate $x$ from equation (3):

$$-3x - y + 2z = 2 \qquad\qquad\qquad (3)$$
$$\underline{3x - 9y + 6z = 42} \qquad\qquad (3) \cdot \text{Eq. (1)}$$
$$-10y + 8z = 44 \qquad\qquad\qquad (6)$$

Solving the system (5), (6) by elimination yields the same solution as above: $(2, -2, 3)$.

## Partial Fraction Decomposition

A rational expression is any quotient of the form $\frac{f}{g}$, where $f$ and $g$ are polynomial expressions. If the degree of $f$ is less than the degree of $g$, the rational expression is called *proper*, otherwise *improper*. An improper rational expression can always be written, using the long division scheme, as a polynomial plus a proper rational expression.

Any polynomial $g$ can, theoretically, be written as the product of one or more linear and quadratic factors, where the quadratic factors have no real zeros (*irreducible* quadratic factors). It follows that any proper rational expression with denominator g can be written as a sum of one or more proper rational expressions, each having a denominator that is a power of a polynomial with degree less than or equal to 2. This sum is called the *partial fraction decomposition* of the rational expression.

**Example 3.4:** $\dfrac{x^2}{x+1}$ is an improper rational expression. It can be rewritten as the sum of a polynomial and a proper rational expression:

$$\frac{x^2}{x+1} = x - 1 + \frac{1}{x+1}.$$

**Example 3.5:** $\dfrac{2x+1}{x^2+x}$ is a proper rational expression. Since its denominator factors as $x^2 + x = x(x + 1)$, the partial fraction decomposition of $\dfrac{2x+1}{x^2+x}$ is $\dfrac{2x+1}{x^2+x} = \dfrac{1}{x} + \dfrac{1}{x+1}$, as can be verified by addition:

$$\frac{1}{x} + \frac{1}{x+1} = \frac{x+1}{x(x+1)} + \frac{x}{x(x+1)} = \frac{2x+1}{x^2+x}$$

**Example 3.6:** $\dfrac{x}{x^2+1}$ is already in partial fraction decomposed form, since the denominator is quadratic and has no real zeros.

A procedure for finding the partial fraction decomposition of a rational expression is:

1. If the expression is proper, go to step 2. If the expression is improper, divide to obtain a polynomial plus a proper rational expression and apply the following steps to the proper expression $f/g$.

2. Write the denominator as a product of powers of linear factors of form $(ax + b)^m$ and irreducible quadratic factors of form $(ax^2 + bx + c)^n$.

3. For each factor $(ax + b)^m$ write a partial fraction sum of form:

$$\frac{A_1}{ax+b} + \frac{A_2}{(ax+b)^2} + \cdots + \frac{A_m}{(ax+b)^m}$$

where the $A_i$ are as yet to be determined unknown coefficients.

4. For each factor $(ax^2 + bx + c)^n$ write a partial fraction sum of form:

$$\frac{B_1 x + C_1}{ax^2 + bx + c} + \frac{B_2 x + C_2}{(ax^2 + bx + c)^2} + \cdots + \frac{B_n x + C_n}{(ax^2 + bx + c)^n}$$

where the $B_j$ and $C_j$ are as yet to be determined unknown coefficients.

5. Set $f/g$ equal to the sum of the partial fractions from steps 4 and 5. Eliminate the denominator $g$ by multiplying both sides to obtain the basic equation for the unknown coefficients.
6. Solve the basic equation for the unknown coefficients.

A general method for solving the basic equation is:
1. Expand both sides.
2. Collect terms in each power of $x$.
3. Equate coefficients of each power of $x$.
4. Solve the linear system in the unknowns $A_i$, $B_j$, and $C_j$ that results.

**Example 3.7:** Find the partial fraction decomposition of $\dfrac{4}{x^2 - 1}$.

This is a proper rational expression. The denominator $x^2 - 1$ factors as $(x - 1)(x + 1)$. Therefore there are only two partial fraction sums, one with denominator $x - 1$ and the other with denominator $x + 1$. Then set

$$\frac{4}{x^2 - 1} = \frac{A_1}{x - 1} + \frac{A_2}{x + 1}$$

Multiply both sides by $x^2 - 1$ to obtain the basic equation

$$4 = A_1(x + 1) + A_2(x - 1)$$

Expanding yields

$$4 = A_1 x + A_1 + A_2 x - A_2$$

Collecting terms in each power of $x$ yields

$$0x + 4 = (A_1 + A_2)x + (A_1 - A_2)$$

For this to hold for all $x$, the coefficients of each power of $x$ on both sides of the equation must be equal; hence:

$$A_1 + A_2 = 0 \text{ (coefficients of } x\text{)}$$
$$A_1 - A_2 = 4 \text{ (constants)}$$

This system has one solution: $A_1 = 2$, $A_2 = -2$. Hence the partial fraction decomposition is

$$\frac{4}{x^2 - 1} = \frac{2}{x - 1} + \frac{-2}{x + 1}$$

## Alternative Method

Instead of expanding both sides of the basic equation, substitute values for $x$ into the equation. If, and only if, all partial fractions have distinct linear denominators, if the values chosen are the distinct zeros of these expressions, the values of the $A_i$ will be found immediately. In other situations there will not be enough of these zeros to determine all the unknowns. Other values of $x$ may be chosen and the resulting system of equations solved, but in these situations the alternative method is not preferred.

**Example 3.8:** Use the alternative method to solve the basic equation in the previous example.

The basic equation is $4 = A_1(x + 1) + A_2(x - 1)$.
Substitute $x = 1$, then it follows that:

$$4 = A_1(1 + 1) + A_2(1 - 1)$$
$$4 = 2A_1$$
$$A_1 = 2$$

Now substitute $x = -1$, then it follows that:

$$4 = A_1(-1 + 1) + A_2(-1 - 1)$$
$$4 = -2A_2$$
$$A_2 = -2$$

This yields the same result as before.

**Example 3.9:** Find the partial fraction decomposition of $\dfrac{2x^3 - 4x}{(x+1)^2(x^2 + 1)}$.

This is a proper rational expression and the denominator is already factored. Notice that $x + 1$ is a repeated linear factor; thus one partial fraction sum must be considered for both $x + 1$ and $(x + 1)^2$. Therefore, there are three partial fraction sums, one each with denominator $x + 1$, $(x + 1)^2$, and $x^2 + 1$. Set

$$\frac{2x^3 - 4x}{(x+1)^2(x^2 + 1)} = \frac{A_1}{x+1} + \frac{A_2}{(x+1)^2} + \frac{B_1x + C_1}{x^2 + 1}$$

Multiply both sides by $(x + 1)^2(x^2 + 1)$ to obtain

$$2x^3 - 4x = A_1(x + 1)(x^2 + 1) + A_2(x^2 + 1) + (B_1x + C_1)(x + 1)^2$$

This is the basic equation. Expanding yields

$$2x^3 - 4x = A_1x^3 + A_1x^2 + A_1x + A_1 + A_2x^2 + A_2$$
$$+ B_1x^3 + 2B_1x^2 + B_1x + C_1x^2 + 2C_1x + C_1$$

Collecting terms in each power of $x$ yields

$$2x^3 + 0x^2 - 4x + 0 = x^3(A_1 + B_1) + x^2(A_1 + A_2 + 2B_1 + C_1)$$
$$+ x(A_1 + B_1 + 2C_1) + (A_1 + A_2 + C_1)$$

For this to hold for all $x$, the coefficients of each power of $x$ on both sides of the equation must be equal, hence:

$$A_1 + B_1 = 2 \quad \text{(coefficients of } x^3)$$
$$A_1 + A_2 + 2B_1 + C_1 = 0 \quad \text{(coefficients of } x^2)$$
$$A_1 + B_1 + 2C_1 = -4 \quad \text{(coefficients of } x)$$
$$A_1 + A_2 + C_1 = 0 \quad \text{(constants)}$$

The only solution to this system is $A_1 = 2, A_2 = 1, B_1 = 0, C_1 = -3$. Hence the partial fraction decomposition is

$$\frac{2x^3 - 4x}{(x+1)^2(x^2+1)} = \frac{2}{x+1} + \frac{1}{(x+1)^2} + \frac{-3}{x^2+1}$$

# Nonlinear Systems of Equations

A system of equations in which any one equation is not linear is a nonlinear system. A nonlinear system may have no solutions, an infinite set of solutions, or any number of real or complex solutions.

Solutions of nonlinear systems in two variables can be found by three methods:

1.  **Graphical method.** Graph each equation. The coordinates of any of the points of intersection may be read from the graph. After checking by substitution in each equation, these coordinates are the real solutions of the system. Normally, only approximations to real solutions can be found by this method, but when the algebraic methods below fail, this method can still be used.
2.  **Substitution method.** Solve one equation for one variable in terms of the other. Substitute this expression into the other equations to determine the value of the first variable. Then substitute this value to determine the value of the other variable.

3. **Elimination method.** Apply the operations on equations leading to equivalent systems to eliminate one variable from one equation, solve the resulting equation for this variable, and substitute this value to determine the value of the other variable.

**Example 3.10:** Solve by substitution:
$$y = x^2 - 2 \quad (1)$$
$$x + 2y = 11 \quad (2).$$

Substitute the expression $x^2 - 2$ from equation (1) into equation (2) for $y$ to obtain $x + 2(x^2 - 2) = 11$.
Solving this quadratic equation in $x$ yields

$$2x^2 + x - 15 = 0$$
$$(2x - 5)(x + 3) = 0$$

$$2x - 5 = 0 \quad \text{or} \quad x + 3 = 0$$
$$x = \frac{5}{2} \qquad\qquad x = -3$$

Substituting these values for $x$ into equation (1) yields:

$$x = \frac{5}{2} : y = \left(\frac{5}{2}\right)^2 - 2 = \frac{17}{4} \qquad x = -3 : y = (-3)^2 - 2 = 7$$

Thus the solutions are $\left(\frac{5}{2}, \frac{17}{4}\right)$ and $(-3, 7)$.

**Example 3.11:** Solve by elimination:
$$x^2 + y^2 = 1 \quad (1)$$
$$x^2 - y^2 = 7 \quad (2).$$

Replacing equation (2) by itself plus equation (1) yields the equivalent system:

$$x^2 + y^2 = 1 \quad (1)$$
$$2x^2 = 8 \quad (3)$$

Solving equation (3) for $x$ yields

$$x^2 = 4$$
$$x = 2 \text{ or } x = -2$$

Substituting these values for $x$ into equation (1) yields:

$$x = 2: \quad 2^2 + y^2 = 1 \qquad x = -2 \quad (-2)^2 + y^2 = 1$$
$$y^2 = -3 \qquad\qquad\qquad y^2 = -3$$
$$y = i\sqrt{3} \quad \text{or} \quad y = -i\sqrt{3} \qquad y = i\sqrt{3} \quad \text{or} \qquad y = -i\sqrt{3}$$

Thus the solutions are $\left(2,i\sqrt{3}\right),\left(2,-i\sqrt{3}\right),\left(-2,i\sqrt{3}\right),\left(-2,-i\sqrt{3}\right).$

There is no general procedure for solving nonlinear systems of equations. Sometimes a combination of the above methods is effective; frequently no algebraic method works and the graphical method can be used to find some approximate solutions, which can then be refined by advanced numerical methods.

# Chapter 4
# ANALYTIC GEOMETRY AND FUNCTIONS

IN THIS CHAPTER:

- ✔ *Analytic Geometry*
- ✔ *Functions*
- ✔ *Algebra of Functions*
- ✔ *Transformations and Graphs*

## Analytic Geometry

A *Cartesian coordinate system* consists of two perpendicular real number lines, called *coordinate axes*, that intersect at their origins. Generally one line is horizontal and called the $x$-axis, and the other is vertical and called the $y$-axis. The axes divide the coordinate plane, or $xy$-plane, into four parts, called *quadrants*, and numbered first, second, third, and fourth, or I, II, III, and IV. Points on the axes are not in any quadrant.

A one-to-one correspondence exists between ordered pairs of numbers $(a, b)$ and points in the coordinate plane (Figure 4-1). Thus,

1. To each point $P$ there corresponds an ordered pair of numbers $(a, b)$ called the coordinates of $P$. $a$ is called the *x-coordinate* or *abscissa*; $b$ is called the *y-coordinate* or *ordinate*.
2. To each ordered pair of numbers there corresponds a point, called the *graph* of the ordered pair. The graph can be indicated by a dot.

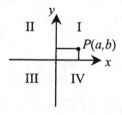

**Figure 4-1**

The distance between two points $P_1(x_1, y_1)$ and $P_2(x_2, y_2)$ in a Cartesian coordinate system is given by the distance formula:

$$d(P_1, P_2) = \sqrt{(x_2 - x_1)^2 + (y_2 - y_1)^2}$$

**Example 4.1:** Find the distance between $(-3, 5)$ and $(4, -1)$.

Label $P_1(x_1, y_1) = (-3, 5)$ and $P_2(x_2, y_2) = (4, -1)$. Then substitute into the distance formula.

$$d(P_1, P_2) = \sqrt{(x_2 - x_1)^2 + (y_2 - y_1)^2}$$
$$= \sqrt{[4 - (-3)]^2 + [(-1) - 5]^2}$$
$$= \sqrt{7^2 + (-6)^2} = \sqrt{85}$$

The *graph* of an equation in two variables is the graph of its solution set, that is, of all ordered pairs $(a, b)$ that satisfy the equation. Since there are ordinarily an infinite number of solutions, a *sketch* of the graph is generally sufficient. A simple approach to finding a sketch of a graph is to find several solutions, plot them, then connect the dots with a smooth curve or line.

**Example 4.2:** Sketch the graph of the equation $x - 2y = 10$.

Form a table of values; then plot the points and connect them. The graph is a straight line, as shown in Figure 4-2.

| $x$ | -2 | 0 | 2 | 4 | 6 | 8 | 10 |
|---|---|---|---|---|---|---|---|
| $y$ | -6 | -5 | -4 | -3 | -2 | -1 | 0 |

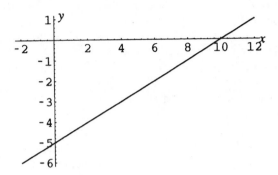

**Figure 4-2**

## Intercepts

The coordinates of the points where the graph of an equation crosses the $x$-axis and $y$-axis have special names:

1. The $x$-coordinate of a point where the graph crosses the $x$-axis is called the $x$-intercept of the graph. To find it, set $y = 0$ and solve for $x$.
2. The $y$-coordinate of a point where the graph crosses the $y$-axis is called the $y$-intercept of the graph. To find it, set $x = 0$ and solve for $y$.

**Example 4.3:** In the previous example, the $x$-intercept of the graph is 10 since the graph crosses the $x$-axis at $(10, 0)$. The $y$-intercept of the graph is $-5$ since the graph crosses the $y$-axis at $(0, -5)$.

**Example 4.4:** Find the intercepts of the graph of $y = 4 - x^2$.

Set $x = 0$; then $y = 4 - 0^2 = 4$. Hence the $y$-intercept is 4.
Set $y = 0$; then $0 = 4 - x^2$, then $x^2 = 4$; thus $x = \pm 2$. Hence 2 and $-2$ are the $x$-intercepts.

## Symmetry

A graph is symmetric with respect to the

1. $y$-axis if $(-a, b)$ is on the graph whenever $(a, b)$ is on the graph.
2. $x$-axis if $(a, -b)$ is on the graph whenever $(a, b)$ is on the graph.
3. origin if $(-a, -b)$ is on the graph whenever $(a, b)$ is on the graph.
4. line $y = x$ if $(b, a)$ is on the graph whenever $(a, b)$ is on the graph.

Tests for symmetry:

1. If substituting $-x$ for $x$ leads to the same equation, the graph has symmetry with respect to the $y$-axis.
2. If substituting $-y$ for $y$ leads to the same equation, the graph has symmetry with respect to the $x$-axis.
3. If simultaneously substituting $-x$ for $x$ and $-y$ for $y$ leads to the same equation, the graph has symmetry with respect to the origin.

   *Note:* It is not possible for a graph to have exactly two of these three symmetries. It must have none, one, or all three symmetries.
4. If interchanging the letters $x$ and $y$ leads to the same equation, the graph has symmetry with respect to the line $y = x$.

**Example 4.5:** Test the equation $y = 4 - x^2$ for symmetry and draw the graph.

Substitute $-x$ for $x$: $y = 4 - (-x)^2 = 4 - x^2$. Since the equation is unchanged, the graph has $y$-axis symmetry (see Figure 4-3).

Substitute $-y$ for $y$: $-y = 4 - x^2$. Since the equation is changed, the graph does not have $x$-axis symmetry.

It is not possible for the graph to have origin symmetry (see note above). Since the graph has $y$-axis symmetry, it is only necessary to find points with nonnegative values of $x$, and then reflect the graph through the $y$-axis.

| $x$ | 0 | 1 | 2 | 3 | 4 |
|-----|---|---|---|----|-----|
| $y$ | 4 | 3 | 0 | -5 | -12 |

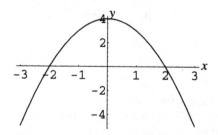

**Figure 4-3**

A circle with center $C(h,k)$ and radius $r > 0$ is the set of all points in the plane that are $r$ units from $C$ (Figure 4-4).

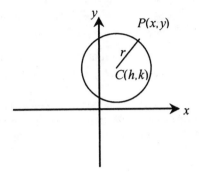

**Figure 4-4**

The equation of a circle with center $C(h,k)$ and radius $r > 0$ can be written as (standard form) $(x - h)^2 + (y - k)^2 = r^2$

If the center of the circle is the origin $(0,0)$, this reduces to $x^2 + y^2 = r^2$.

If $r = 1$ the circle is called a *unit circle*.

# Functions

A *function f* from set $D$ to set $E$ is a rule or correspondence that assigns to each element $x$ of set $D$ exactly one element $y$ of set $E$. The set $D$ is called the *domain* of the function. The element $y$ of $E$ is called the *image* of $x$ under $f$, or the value of $f$ at $x$, and is written $f(x)$. The subset $R$ of $E$ consisting of all images of elements of $D$ is called the range of the function. The members of the domain $D$ and range $R$ are referred to as the input and output values, respectively.

**Example 4.6:** Let $D$ be the set of all words in English having fewer than 20 letters. Let $f$ be the rule that assigns to each word the number of letters in the word. Then $E$ can be the set of all integers; $R$ is the set $\{x \in \mathbf{N} | 1 \le x < 20\}$ (i.e., the set of natural numbers less than 20). $f$ assigns to the word "truth" the number 5; this would be written $f(\text{truth}) = 5$. Moreover, $f(a) = 1, f(\text{right}) = 5$, and $f(\text{president}) = 9$.

**Example 4.7:** Let $D$ be the set of real numbers and $g$ be the rule given by

$g(x) = x^2 + 3$. Find: $g(4)$, $g(-4)$, $g(a) + g(b)$, $g(a + b)$. What is the range of $g$?

$$g(4) = 4^2 + 3 = 16 + 3 = 19 \quad g(-4) = (-4)2 + 3 = 16 + 3 = 19$$
$$g(a) + g(b) = a^2 + 3 + b^2 + 3 = a^2 + b^2 + 6$$
$$g(a + b) = (a + b)^2 + 3 = a^2 + 2ab + b^2 + 3$$

The range of $g$ is found by noting that the square of a number is always greater than or equal to zero; hence $g(x) = x^2 + 3 \geq 3$. Thus, the range of $g$ is $\{y \in \mathbf{R} \mid y \geq 3\}$.

A function is indicated by the notation $f: D \to E$. The effect of a function on an element of $D$ is then written $f: x \to f(x)$. A picture of the type shown in Figure 4-5 is often used to visualize the function relationship.

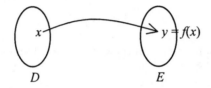

**Figure 4-5**

The domain and range of a function are normally sets of real numbers. If a function is defined by an expression and the domain is not stated, the domain is assumed to be the set of all real numbers for which the expression is defined. This set is called the *implied domain*, or the *largest possible domain*, of the function.

**Example 4.8:** Find the (largest possible) domain for

(a) $f(x) = \dfrac{x-3}{x+6}$  (b) $g(x) = \sqrt{x-5}$  (c) $h(x) = x^2 - 4$.

(a) The expression $\dfrac{x-3}{x+6}$ is defined for all real numbers $x$ except when $x + 6 = 0$, that is, when $x = -6$. Thus the domain of $f$ is $\{x \in \mathbf{R} \mid x \neq -6\}$.

(b) The expression $\sqrt{x-5}$ is defined when $x - 5 \geq 0$, that is, when $x \geq 5$. Thus the domain of $g$ is $\{x \in \mathbf{R} \mid x \geq 5\}$.

(c) The expression $x^2 - 4$ is defined for all real numbers. Thus the domain of $h$ is $\mathbf{R}$.

## You Need to Know

The graph of a function $f$ is the graph of all points $(x, y)$ such that $x$ is in the domain of $f$, and $y = f(x)$.

## The Vertical Line Test

Since for each value of $x$ in the domain of $f$ there is exactly one value of $y$ such that $y = f(x)$, a vertical line $x = c$ can cross the graph of a function at most once. Thus, if a vertical line crosses a graph more than once, the graph is not the graph of a function.

## Increasing, Decreasing, and Constant Functions

1. If, for all $x$ in an interval, as $x$ increases, the value of $f(x)$ increases; thus, the graph of the function rises from left to right, then the function $f$ is called an *increasing function on the interval*. A function that is increasing throughout its domain is referred to as an *increasing function*.

2. If, for all $x$ in an interval, as $x$ increases, the value of $f(x)$ decreases; thus, the graph of the function falls from left to right, then the function $f$ is called a *decreasing function on the interval*. A function that is decreasing throughout its domain is referred to as a *decreasing function*.

3. If the value of a function does not change on an interval, thus, the graph of a function is a horizontal line segment, then the function is called a *constant function on the interval*. A function that is constant throughout its domain is referred to as a *constant function*.

**Example 4.9:** Given the graph of $f(x)$ shown in Figure 4-6, assuming the domain of $f$ is **R**, identify the intervals on which $f$ is increasing or decreasing:

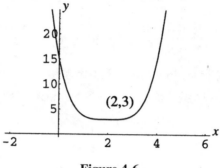

**Figure 4-6**

As $x$ increases through the domain of $f$, $y$ decreases until $x = 2$, then increases. Thus the function is decreasing on $(-\infty, 2)$ and increasing on $(2, \infty)$.

## Even and Odd Functions

1. If, for all $x$ in the domain of a function $f$, $f(-x) = f(x)$, the function is called an even function. Since, for an even function, the equation $y = f(x)$ is not changed when $-x$ is substituted for $x$, the graph of an even function has $y$-axis symmetry.

2. If, for all $x$ in the domain of a function $f$, $f(-x) = -f(x)$, the function is called an odd function. Since, for an odd function, the equation $y = f(x)$ is not changed when $-x$ is substituted for $x$ and $-y$ is substituted for $y$, the graph of an odd function has origin symmetry.

## Remember

Most functions are neither even nor odd.

**Example 4.10:** Determine whether the following functions are even, odd, or neither:

$(a)\, f(x) = 7x^2$  $(b)\, g(x) = 4x + 6$  $(c)\, h(x) = 6x - \sqrt[3]{x}$  $(d)\, F(x) = \dfrac{4}{x - 6}$

(a) Consider $f(-x)$. $f(-x) = 7(-x)^2 = 7x^2$. Since $f(-x) = f(x)$, $f$ is an even function.

(b) Consider $g(-x)$. $g(-x) = 4(-x) + 6 = -4x + 6$. Also $-g(x) = -(4x + 6) = -4x - 6$. Since neither $g(-x) = g(x)$ nor $g(-x) = -g(x)$ is the case, the function $g$ is neither even nor odd.

(c) Consider $h(-x)$. $h(-x) = 6(-x) - \sqrt[3]{-x} = -6x + \sqrt[3]{x}$. Thus, $h(-x) = -h(x)$ and $h$ is an odd function.

(d) Consider $F(-x)$. $F(-x) = \dfrac{4}{-x-6} = -\dfrac{4}{x+6}$. Since neither $F(-x) = F(x)$ nor $F(-x) = -F(x)$ is the case, the function $F$ is neither even nor odd.

In applications, if $y = f(x)$, the language "$y$ is a function of $x$" is used. $x$ is referred to as the independent variable, and $y$ as the dependent variable.

**Example 4.11:** In the formula $A = \pi r^2$, the area $A$ of a circle is written as a function of the radius $r$. To write the radius as a function of the area, solve this equation for $r$ in terms of $A$, thus:

$$r^2 = \frac{A}{\pi}, \quad r = \pm\sqrt{\frac{A}{\pi}}.$$

Since the radius is positive, $r = \sqrt{\dfrac{A}{\pi}}$ gives $r$ as a function of $A$.

## Algebra of Functions

Algebraic combinations of functions can be obtained in several ways. Given two functions $f$ and $g$, the sum, difference, product, and quotient functions can be defined as follows:

| Name | Definition | Domain |
|---|---|---|
| Sum | $(f + g)(x) = f(x) + g(x)$ | The set of all $x$ that are in the domain of both $f$ and $g$ |
| Difference | $(f - g)(x) = f(x) - g(x)$ | The set of all $x$ that are in the domain of both $f$ and $g$ |
| Product | $(fg)(x) = f(x)g(x)$ | The set of all $x$ that are in the domain of both $f$ and $g$ |
| Quotient | $\left(\dfrac{f}{g}\right)(x) = \dfrac{f(x)}{g(x)}$ | The set of all $x$ that are in the domain of both $f$ and $g$, with $g(x) \neq 0$. |

**Example 4.12:** Given $f(x) = x^2$ and $g(x) = \sqrt{x-2}$, find $(f+g)(x)$ and $(f/g)(x)$ and state the domains of the functions.

$(f+g)(x) = f(x) + g(x) = x^2 + \sqrt{x-2}$. Since the domain of $f$ is $\mathbf{R}$ and the domain of $g$ is $\{x \in \mathbf{R} \mid x \geq 2\}$ the domain of this function is also $\{x \in \mathbf{R} \mid x \geq 2\}$.

$\left(\dfrac{f}{g}\right)(x) = \dfrac{f(x)}{g(x)} = \dfrac{x^2}{\sqrt{x-2}}$. The domain of this function is the same as the domain of $f+g$, with the further restriction that $g(x) \neq 0$, that is, $\{x \in \mathbf{R} \mid x > 2\}$.

The composite function $f \circ g$ of two functions $f$ and $g$ is defined by: $f \circ g(x) = f(g(x))$.

The domain of $f \circ g$ is the set of all $x$ in the domain of $g$ such that $g(x)$ is in the domain of $f$.

**Example 4.13:** Given $f(x) = x^2$ and $g(x) = \sqrt{x-5}$, find $f \circ g$ and state its domain.

$f \circ g(x) = f(g(x)) = f\left(\sqrt{x-5}\right) = \left(\sqrt{x-5}\right)^2 = x - 5$. The domain of $f \circ g$ is not all of $\mathbf{R}$. Since the domain of $g$ is $\{x \in \mathbf{R} \mid x \geq 5\}$, the domain of $f \circ g$ is the set of all $x \geq 5$ in the domain of $f$, that is, all of $\{x \in \mathbf{R} \mid x \geq 5\}$.

Figure 4-7 shows the relationship among $f$, $g$, and $f \circ g$.

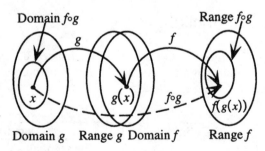

**Figure 4-7**

## One-To-One Functions

A function with domain $D$ and range $R$ is called a *one-to-one* function if exactly one element of set $D$ corresponds to each element of set $R$.

A function with domain $D$ and range $R$ is *one-to-one* if either of the following equivalent conditions is satisfied.

1. Whenever $f(u) = f(v)$ in $R$, then $u = v$ in $D$.
2. Whenever $u \neq v$ in $D$, then $f(u) \neq f(v)$ in $R$.

**Example 4.14:** Let $f(x) = x^2$ and $g(x) = 2x$. Show that $f$ is not a one-to-one function and that $g$ is a one-to-one function.
The domain of $f$ is **R**. Since $f(3) = f(-3) = 9$, $f$ is not one-to-one.

The domain and range of $g$ are both **R**. Let $k$ be an arbitrary real number. If $2x = k$, then the only $x$ that corresponds to $k$ is $x = k/2$. Thus $g$ is one-to-one.

Since for each value of $y$ in the domain of a one-to-one function $f$ there is exactly one $x$ such that $y = f(x)$, a horizontal line $y = c$ can cross the graph of a one-to-one function at most once. Thus, if a horizontal line crosses a graph more than once, the graph is not the graph of a one-to-one function. This is known as the *horizontal line test*.

## Inverse Functions

Let $f$ be a one-to-one function with domain $D$ and range $R$. Since for each $y$ in $R$ there is exactly one $x$ in $D$ such that $y = f(x)$, define a function $g$ with domain $R$ and range $D$ such that $g(y) = x$. Then $g$ reverses the correspondence defined by $f$. The function $g$ is called the inverse function of $f$ and is often denoted $f^{-1}$.

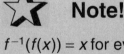 **Note!**

$$f^{-1}(f(x)) = x \text{ for every } x \text{ in } D$$
$$\text{and}$$
$$f(f^{-1}(y)) = y \text{ for every } y \text{ in } R.$$

To find the inverse function for a given function $f$:
1. Verify that $f$ is one-to-one.
2. Solve the equation $y = f(x)$ for $x$ in terms of $y$, if possible. This gives an equation of form $x = f^{-1}(y)$.
3. Interchange $x$ and $y$ in the equation found in step 2. This gives an equation of the form $y = f^{-1}(x)$.

**Example 4.15:** Find the inverse function for $f(x) = \dfrac{2}{x+3}$.

First show that $f$ is one-to-one. Assume $f(u) = f(v)$. Then:

$$\frac{2}{u+3} = \frac{2}{v+3}$$

$$(u+3)(v+3) \cdot \frac{2}{u+3} = \frac{2}{v+3} \cdot (u+3)(v+3)$$

$$2(v+3) = 2(u+3)$$

$$2v+6 = 2u+6$$

$$2v = 2u$$

$$v = u$$

Thus, $f$ is one-to-one. Now solve $y = \dfrac{2}{x+3}$ for $x$ to obtain

$$y(x+3) = 2$$

$$yx + 3y = 2$$

$$yx = 2 - 3y$$

$$x = \frac{2}{y} - 3$$

Now interchange $x$ and $y$ to obtain $y = f^{-1}(x) = \dfrac{2}{y} - 3$.

The graphs of $y = f(x)$ and $y = f^{-1}(x)$ are symmetric with respect to the line $y = x$.

# Transformations and Graphs

The graphs of many functions can be regarded as arising from more basic graphs as a result of one or more elementary transformations. The elementary transformations considered here are: shifting, stretching and compression, and reflection with respect to a coordinate axis.

Given a basic function $y = f(x)$ with a graph shown in Figure 4-8, the following transformations have easily identified effects on the graph.

## Vertical Shifting

The graph of $y = f(x) + k$, for $k > 0$, is the same as the graph of $y = f(x)$ *shifted up* $k$ units. The graph of $y = f(x) - k$, for $k > 0$, is the same as the graph of $y = f(x)$ *shifted down* $k$ units.

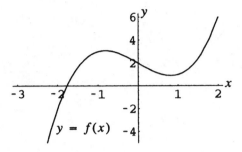

**Figure 4-8**

**Example 4.16:** For the basic function shown in Figure 4-8, graph $y = f(x)$ and $y = f(x) + 2$ on the same coordinate system (Figure 4-9) and $y = f(x)$ and $y = f(x) - 2.5$ on the same coordinate system (Figure 4-10).

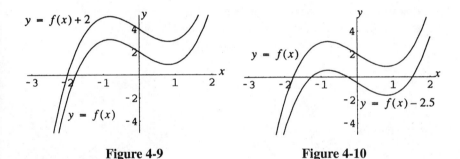

**Figure 4-9**                **Figure 4-10**

## Vertical Stretching and Compression

The graph of $y = af(x)$, for $a > 1$, is the same as the graph of $y = f(x)$ *stretched*, with respect to the y-axis, by a factor of $a$. The graph of $y = af(x)$, for $0 < a < 1$, is the same as the graph of $y = f(x)$ *compressed*, with respect to the y-axis, by a factor of $1/a$.

**Example 4.17:** For the basic function shown in Figure 4-8, graph $y = f(x)$ and $y = 2f(x)$ on the same coordinate system (Figure 4-11); $y = f(x)$ and $y = 1/3f(x)$ on the same coordinate system (Figure 4-12).

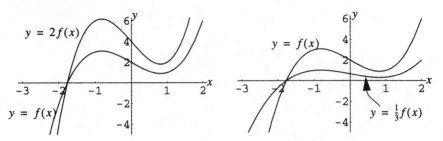

**Figure 4-11**                    **Figure 4-12**

## Horizontal Shifting

The graph of $y = f(x + h)$, for $h > 0$, is the same as the graph of $y = f(x)$ *shifted left h units*. The graph of $y = f(x - h)$, for $h > 0$, is the same as the graph of $y = f(x)$ *shifted right h units*.

**Example 4.18:** For the basic function shown in Figure 4-8, graph $y = f(x)$ and $y = f(x + 2)$ on the same coordinate system (Figure 4-13); $y = f(x)$ and $y = f(x - 1)$ on the same coordinate system (Figure 4-14).

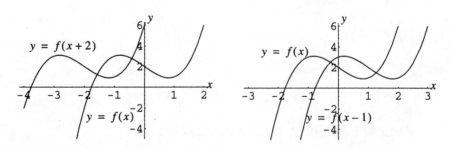

**Figure 4-13**                    **Figure 4-14**

## Horizontal Stretching and Compression

The graph of $y = f(ax)$, for $a > 1$, is the same as the graph of $y = f(x)$ *compressed*, with respect to the x-axis, by a factor of $a$. The graph of $y = f(ax)$, for $0 < a < 1$, is the same as the graph of $y = f(x)$ *stretched*, with respect to the x-axis, by a factor of $1/a$.

**Example 4.19:** For the basic function shown in Figure 4-8, graph $y = f(x)$ and $y = f(2x)$ on the same coordinate system (Figure 4-15); $y = f(x)$ and $y = f(1/2x)$ on the same coordinate system (Figure 4-16).

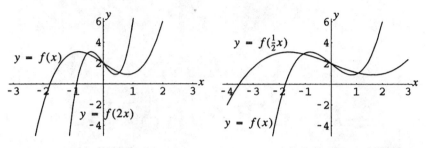

**Figure 4-15**                    **Figure 4-16**

## Reflection with Respect to a Coordinate Axis

The graph of $y = -f(x)$ is the same as the graph of $y = f(x)$ *reflected across the x-axis.* The graph of $y = f(-x)$ is the same as the graph of $y = f(x)$ reflected across the y-axis.

**Example 4.20:** For the basic function shown in Figure 4-8, graph $y = f(x)$ and $y = -f(x)$ on the same coordinate system (Figure 4-17); $y = f(x)$ and $y = f(-x)$ on the same coordinate system (Figure 4-18).

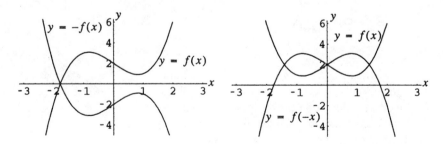

**Figure 4-17**                    **Figure 4-18**

# Chapter 5
# ALGEBRAIC FUNCTIONS AND THEIR GRAPHS

<small>IN THIS CHAPTER</small>

- ✔ *Linear Functions*
- ✔ *Quadratic Functions*
- ✔ *Polynomial Functions*
- ✔ *Division of Polynomials*
- ✔ *Rational Functions*

## Linear Functions

A *linear function* is any function specified by a rule of the form $f: x \rightarrow mx + b$, where $m \neq 0$. If $m = 0$, the function is not considered to be a linear function; a function $f(x) = b$ is called a *constant function*. The graph of a linear function is always a straight line. The graph of a constant function is a horizontal straight line.

The slope of a line that is not parallel to the $y$-axis is defined as follows: Let $(x_1, y_1)$ and $(x_2, y_2)$ be distinct points on the line. Then the slope of the line is given by

$$m = \frac{y_2 - y_1}{x_2 - x_1} = \frac{\text{change in } y}{\text{change in } x} = \frac{\text{rise}}{\text{run}}$$

**Example 5.1:** Find the slope of the lines through (*a*) (5,3) and (8,12) *(b)*
(3,– 4) and (–5,6).
   (*a*)  Identify $(x_1,y_1) = (5,3)$ and $(x_2,y_2) = (8,12)$. Then

$$m = \frac{y_2 - y_1}{x_2 - x_1} = \frac{12 - 3}{8 - 5} = 3$$

   (*b*)  Identify $(x_1,y_1) = (3,- 4)$ and $(x_2,y_2) = (-5,6)$. Then

$$m = \frac{y_2 - y_1}{x_2 - x_1} = \frac{6 - (-4)}{-5 - 3} = -\frac{5}{4}$$

## Horizontal and Vertical Lines

A *horizontal line* (a line parallel to the *x*-axis) has slope 0, since any two
points on the line have the same y coordinates. A horizontal line has an
equation of the form $y = k$.

   A vertical line (a line parallel to the *y*-axis) has undefined slope, since
any two points on the line have the same *x* coordinates. A vertical line has
an equation of the form $x = h$.

   The equation of a line can be written in several forms. Among the
most useful are:

1.   *Slope-Intercept Form:* The equation of a line with slope *m* and
      *y*-intercept *b* is given by $y = mx + b$.
2.   *Point-Slope Form:* The equation of a line passing through
      $(x_0,y_0)$ with slope *m* is given by $y - y_0 = m(x - x_0)$.
3.   *Standard Form:* The equation of a line can be written as $Ax + By$
      $= C$, where *A, B, C* are integers with no common factors; *A* and
      *B* are not both zero.

**Example 5.2:** Find the equation of the line passing through (−6,4) with
slope 2/3.

Use the point-slope form of the equation: $y - 4 = 2/3[x - (-6)]$. This can
then be simplified to slope-intercept form: $y = 2/3x + 8$. In standard form
this would become $2x - 3y = -24$.

## Parallel and Perpendicular Lines

If two nonvertical lines are parallel, their slopes are equal. Conversely, if
two lines have the same slope, they are parallel; two vertical lines are also
parallel.

**Example 5.3:** Find the equation of a line through $(3, -8)$ parallel to $5x + 2y = 7$.

First find the slope of the given line by isolating the variable $y$: $y = -\dfrac{5}{2}x + \dfrac{7}{2}$. Thus the given line has slope $-\dfrac{5}{2}$. Hence the desired line has slope $-\dfrac{5}{2}$ and passes through $(3, -8)$. Use the point-slope form to obtain $y - (-8) = -\dfrac{5}{2}(x - 3)$, which is written in standard form as $5x + 2y = -1$.

If a line is horizontal, any line perpendicular to it is vertical, and conversely. If two nonvertical lines, with slopes $m_1$ and $m_2$, are perpendicular, then their slopes satisfy $m_1 m_2 = -1$ or $m_2 = -1/m_1$.

**Example 5.4:** Find the equation of a line through $(3, -8)$ perpendicular to $5x + 2y = 7$.

The given line was found in the previous example to have slope $-\dfrac{5}{2}$. Hence the desired line has slope $\dfrac{2}{5}$ and passes through $(3, -8)$. Use the point-slope form to obtain $y - (-8) = \dfrac{2}{5}(x - 3)$, which is written in standard form as $2x - 5y = 46$.

## Quadratic Functions

A *quadratic function* is any function specified by a rule that can be written as $f : x \rightarrow ax^2 + bx + c$, where $a \neq 0$. The form $ax^2 + bx + c$ is called *standard* form.

**Example 5.5:** $f(x) = x^2$, and $f(x) = 3x^2 - 2x + 15$ are examples of quadratic functions. $f(x) = 3x + 5$ and $f(x) = x^3$ are examples of nonquadratic functions.

The basic quadratic function is the function $f(x) = x^2$. The graph of $f(x)$ is a parabola with vertex at the origin $(0,0)$ and axis of symmetry the $y$-axis (Figure 5-1).

$$y = x^2$$

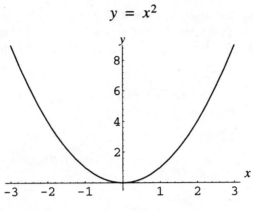

**Figure 5-1**

Any quadratic function can be written in the form $f(x) = a(x - h)^2 + k$ by completing the square. Therefore, any quadratic function has a graph that can be regarded as the result of performing simple transformations on the graph of the basic function $f(x) = x^2$. Thus the graph of any quadratic function is a parabola.

**Example 5.6:** The quadratic function $f(x) = 2x^2 - 12x + 4$ can be rewritten as follows:

$$f(x) = 2x^2 - 12x + 4$$
$$= 2(x^2 - 6x) + 4$$
$$= 2(x^2 - 6x + 9) - 9 \cdot 2 + 4$$
$$= 2(x - 3)^2 - 14$$

The graph of the function $f(x) = a(x - h)^2 + k$, for positive $a$, is the same as the graph of the basic quadratic function $f(x) = x^2$ stretched by a factor of $a$ (if $a > 1$) or compressed by a factor of $1/a$ (if $0 < a < 1$), and shifted left, right, up, or down so that the point $(0,0)$ becomes the vertex $(h,k)$ of the new graph. The graph of $f(x) = a(x - h)^2 + k$ is symmetric with respect to the line $x = h$. The graph is referred to as a parabola opening *up*. The function has a *minimum* value of $k$ attained when $x = h$.

If $a$ is negative, the graph of the function $f(x) = a(x - h)^2 + k$ is the same as the graph of the basic quadratic function $f(x) = -x^2$ stretched by a factor of $|a|$ (if $|a| > 1$) or compressed by a factor of $1/|a|$ (if $0 < |a| < 1$), and shifted left, right, up, or down so that the point $(0,0)$ becomes the vertex $(h,k)$ of the new graph. The graph of $f(x) = a(x - h)^2 + k$ is symmetric with respect to the line $x = h$. The graph is referred to as a parabola opening *down*. The function has a *maximum* value of $k$ attained when $x = h$.

**Example 5.7:** Consider the function $f(x) = x^2 + 4x - 7$. By completing the square, this can be written as

$$f(x) = x^2 + 4x + 4 - 4 - 7 = (x + 2)^2 - 11.$$

Thus the graph of the function is the same as the graph of $f(x)$ shifted left 2 units and down 11 units; see Figure 5-2.

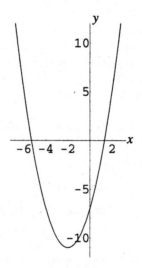

**Figure 5-2**

The graph is a parabola with vertex $(-2, -11)$, opening up. The function has a minimum value of $-11$. This minimum value is attained when $x = -2$.

**Example 5.8:** Consider the function $f(x) = 6x - x^2$. By completing the square, this can be written as $f(x) = x^2 + 6x = -(x^2 - 6x + 9) + 9 = -(x - 3)^2 + 9$. Thus the graph of the function is the same as the graph of $f(x) = -x^2$ shifted right 3 units and up 9 units. The graph is shown in Figure 5-3.

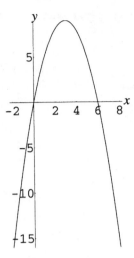

**Figure 5-3**

The graph is a parabola with vertex (3,9), opening down. The function has a maximum value of 9. This value is attained when $x = 3$.

## Polynomial Functions

A polynomial function is any function specified by a rule that can be written as $f : x \rightarrow a_n x^n + a_{n-1} x^{n-1} + \cdots + a_1 x + a_0$, where $a_n \neq 0$. $n$ is the degree of the polynomial function. The domain of a polynomial function, unless otherwise specified, is $R$.

Special polynomial functions such as constant functions ($f(x) = a_0$), linear functions ($f(x) = a_1 x + a_0$) and quadratic functions ($f(x) = a_2 x^2 + a_1 x + a_0$) have already been discussed.

If $f$ has degree $n$ and all coefficients except $a_n$ are zero then $f(x) = ax^n$, where $a = a_n \neq 0$. Then if $n$ is an odd integer, the function is an odd function. If $n$ is an even integer, the function is an even function.

**Example 5.9:** Draw graphs of (a) $f(x) = x^3$; (b) $f(x) = x^5$; (c) $f(x) = x^4$; (d) $f(x) = x^6$.

(*a*) Figure 5-4; (*b*) Figure 5-5; (*c*) Figure 5-6; (*d*) Figure 5-7.

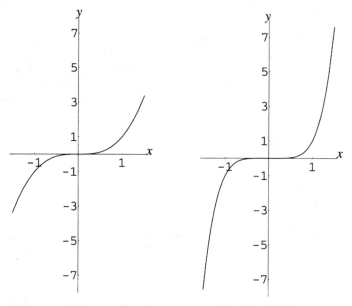

Figure 5-4

Figure 5-5

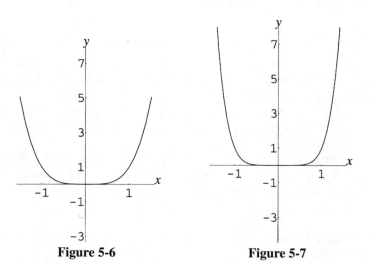

Figure 5-6

Figure 5-7

## Division of Polynomials

If a polynomial $g(x)$ is a factor of another polynomial $f(x)$, then $f(x)$ is said to be divisible by $g(x)$. Thus $x^3 - 1$ is divisible both by $x - 1$ and $x^2 + x + 1$. If a polynomial is not divisible by another, it is possible to apply the technique of long division to find a quotient and remainder, as in the following example:

**Example 5.10:** Find the quotient and remainder for $(2x^4 - x^2 - 2)/(x^2 + 2x - 1)$.

(1) Divide the first term of the dividend by the first term of the divisor.
(2) Multiply the divisor by $2x^2$ and subtract.
(3) Bring down the next term; repeat the division step.
(4) Multiply the divisor by $-4x$ and subtract.
(5) Bring down the next term and repeat the division step.
(6) Multiply the divisor by 9 and subtract.
(7) The remainder; the degree is less than the degree of the divisor.

$$
\begin{array}{r}
2x^2 \;-\; 4x \;+\; 9 \\
x^2 + 2x - 1 \overline{\smash{\big)}\; 2x^4 \;+\; 0x^3 \;-\; x^2 \;+\; 0x \;-\; 2} \\
\underline{-(2x^4 \;+\; 4x^3 \;-\; 2x^2)} \\
-\;4x^3 \;+\; x^2 \;+\; 0x \\
\underline{-(-4x^3 \;-\; 8x^2 \;+\; 4x)} \\
9x^2 \;-\; 4x \;-\; 2 \\
\underline{-(9x^2 \;+\; 18x \;-\; 9)} \\
-\;22x \;+\; 7
\end{array}
$$

(1)
(2)
(3)
(4)
(5)
(6)
(7)

The quotient is $2x^2 - 4x + 9$ and the remainder is $-22x + 7$. Thus:

$$\frac{2x^4 - x^2 - 2}{x^2 + 2x - 1} = 2x^2 - 4x + 9 + \frac{-22x + 7}{x^2 + 2x - 1}$$

If $f(x)$ and $g(x)$ are polynomials, with $g(x) \neq 0$, then there exist unique polynomials $q(x)$ and $r(x)$ such that

$$f(x) = g(x)q(x) + r(x) \quad \text{and} \quad \frac{f(x)}{g(x)} = q(x) + \frac{r(x)}{g(x)}$$

Either $r(x) = 0$ ($f(x)$ is divisible by $g(x)$) or the degree of $r(x)$ is less than the degree of $g(x)$.

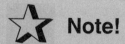

## Note!

When the polynomial $f(x)$ is divided by $x - c$, the remainder is $f(c)$.

## Synthetic Division

Division of a polynomial $f(x)$ by a polynomial of form $x - c$ is accomplished efficiently by the synthetic division scheme. Arrange coefficients of the dividend $f(x)$ in descending order in the first row of a three-row array.

$$c \mid a_n \quad a_{n-1} \quad \cdots \quad a_1 \quad a_0$$

The third row is formed by bringing down the first coefficient of $f(x)$, then successively multiplying each coefficient in the third row by $c$, placing the result in the second row, adding this to the corresponding coefficient in the first row, and placing the result in the next position in the third row.

$$
\begin{array}{c|ccccc}
c & a_n & a_{n-1} & \cdots & a_1 & a_0 \\
  &     & ca_n & cb_1 & \cdots & cb_{n-2} & cb_{n-1} \\
\hline
  & a_n & b_1 & \cdots & b_{n-1} & r
\end{array}
$$

The last coefficient in the third row is the constant remainder; the other coefficients are the coefficients of the quotient, in descending order.

**Example 5.11:** Use synthetic division to find the quotient and remainder in the previous example. In this case, $c = 4$. Arrange the coefficients of $x^3 - 5x^2 + 7x - 9$ in the first row of a three-row array; proceed to bring down the first coefficient, 1, then multiply by 4, place result in second row, add to $-5$, place result in third row. Continue to the last coefficient of the array.

$$
\begin{array}{c|cccc}
4 & 1 & -5 & 7 & -9 \\
  &   & 4 & -4 & 12 \\
\hline
  & 1 & -1 & 3 & 3
\end{array}
$$

The quotient is $x^2 - x + 3$ and the remainder is the constant 3. Thus

$$\frac{x^3 - 5x^2 + 7x - 9}{x - 4} = x^2 - x + 3 + \frac{3}{x - 4}$$

## Theorems about Zeros

If $f(c) = 0$, $c$ is called a *zero* of the polynomial $f(x)$.

1. A polynomial $f(x)$ has a factor of $x - c$ if and only if $f(c) = 0$. Thus, $x - c$ is a factor of a polynomial if and only if $c$ is a zero of the polynomial.

2. If $P(x)$ is a polynomial with real coefficients, and if $z$ is a complex zero of $P(x)$, then the complex conjugate $\bar{z}$ is also a zero of $P(x)$. That is, complex zeros of polynomials with real coefficients occur in complex conjugate pairs.

3. Any polynomial of degree $n > 0$ with real coefficients has a complete factorization using linear and quadratic factors, multiplied by the leading coefficient of the polynomial. However, it is not necessarily possible to find the factorization using exact algebraic methods.

4. If $P(x) = a_n x^n + a_{n-1} x^{n-1} + \cdots + a_1 x + a_0$ is a polynomial with integral coefficients and $r = p/q$ is a rational zero of $P(x)$ in lowest terms, then $p$ must be a factor of the constant term $a_0$ and $q$ must be a factor of the leading coefficient $a_n$.

**Example 5.12:** Find a polynomial of least degree with real coefficients and zeros 2 and $1 - 3i$.

By the factor theorem, $c$ is a zero of a polynomial only if $x - c$ is a factor. By the theorem on zeros of polynomials with real coefficients, if $1 - 3i$ is a zero of this polynomial, then so is $1 + 3i$. Hence the polynomial can be written as

$$P(x) = a(x - 2)[(x - (1 - 3i)][(x - (1 + 3i)]$$

Simplifying yields:

$$P(x) = a(x - 2)[(x - 1) + 3i][(x - 1) - 3i]$$
$$= a(x - 2)[(x - 1)^2 - (3i)^2]$$
$$= a(x - 2)(x^2 - 2x + 10)$$
$$= a(x^3 - 4x^2 + 14x - 20)$$

**Example 5.13:** List the possible rational zeros of $3x^2 + 5x - 8$.

From the theorem on rational zeros of polynomials with integer coefficients, the possible rational zeros are:

$$\frac{\text{Factors of } -8}{\text{Factors of } 3} = \frac{\pm 1, \pm 2, \pm 4, \pm 8}{\pm 1, \pm 3} = \pm 1, \pm 2, \pm 4, \pm 8, \pm \frac{1}{3}, \pm \frac{2}{3}, \pm \frac{4}{3}, \pm \frac{8}{3}$$

Note that the actual zeros are 1 and $-\frac{8}{3}$.

## Theorems Used in Locating Zeros

1.  *Intermediate Value Theorem*: Given a polynomial $f(x)$ with $a <$ $b$, if $f(a) \neq f(b)$, then $f(x)$ takes on every value $c$ between $a$ and $b$ in the interval $(a,b)$.
2.  *Corollary*: For a polynomial $f(x)$, if $f(a)$ and $f(b)$ have opposite signs, then $f(x)$ has at least one zero between $a$ and $b$.
3.  *Descartes's Rule of Signs:* If $f(x)$ is a polynomial with terms arranged in descending order, then the number of positive real zeros of $f(x)$ is either equal to the number of sign changes between successive terms of $f(x)$ or is less than this number by an even number. The number of negative real zeros of $f(x)$ is found by applying this rule to $f(-x)$.
4.  If the third line of a synthetic division of $f(x)$ by $x - r$ is all positive for some $r > 0$, then $r$ is an upper bound for the zeros of $f$ $(x)$; that is, there are no zeros greater than $r$. If the terms in the third line of a synthetic division of $f(x)$ by $x - r$ alternate signs for some $r < 0$, then $r$ is a lower bound for the zeros of $f(x)$; that is, there are no zeros less than $r$. (0 may be regarded as positive or negative for the purpose of this theorem.)

> **The following statements are equivalent:**
> 1.  $c$ is a zero of $P(x)$.
> 2.  $c$ is a solution of the equation $P(x) = 0$.
> 3.  $x - c$ is a factor of $P(x)$.
> 4.  For real $c$, the graph of $y = P(x)$ has an $x$-intercept at $c$.

To graph a polynomial function for which all factors can be found:
1. Write the polynomial in factored form.
2. Determine the sign behavior of the polynomial from the signs of the factors.
3. Enter the $x$-intercepts of the polynomial on the $x$-axis.
4. If desired, form a table of values.
5. Sketch the graph of the polynomial as a smooth curve.

**Example 5.14:** Sketch a graph of $y = 2x(x - 3)(x + 2)$.

The polynomial is already in factored form. Use the methods of Chapter 2 to obtain the sign chart shown in Figure 5-8.

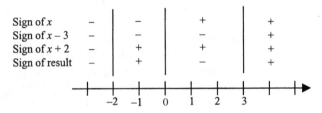

**Figure 5-8**

The graph has $x$-intercepts $-2$, $0$, $3$ and is below the $x$-axis on the intervals $(-\infty, -2)$ and $(0,3)$ and above the $x$-axis on the intervals $(-2,0)$ and $(3, \infty)$. Form a table of values as shown and sketch the graph as a smooth curve (Figure 5-9).

| $x$ | $-3$ | $-2$ | $-1$ | 0 | 1 | 2 | 3 | 4 |
|---|---|---|---|---|---|---|---|---|
| $y$ | $-36$ | 0 | 8 | 0 | $-12$ | $-16$ | 0 | 48 |

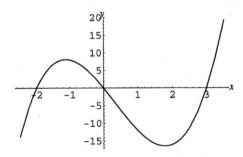

**Figure 5-9**

# Rational Functions

A rational function is any function which can be specified by a rule written as $f(x) = \dfrac{P(x)}{Q(x)}$, where $P(x)$ and $Q(x)$ are polynomial functions. The domain of a rational function is the set of all real numbers for which $Q(x) \neq 0$. The assumption is normally made that the rational expression $P(x)/Q(x)$ is in lowest terms, that is, $P(x)$ and $Q(x)$ have no factors in common.

**Example 5.15:**

$$f(x) = \frac{12}{x}, \quad g(x) = \frac{x^2}{x^2-9}, \quad h(x) = \frac{(x+1)(x-4)}{x(x-2)(x+3)}, \quad \text{and } k(x) = \frac{3x}{x^2+4}$$

are examples of rational functions. The domains are, respectively, for $f$, $\{x \in R \mid x \neq 0\}$, for $g$, $\{x \in R \mid x \neq \pm 3\}$, for $h$, $\{x \in R \mid x \neq 0,2,-3\}$, and for $k$, $R$ (since the denominator polynomial is never 0).

The graph of a rational function is analyzed in terms of the symmetry, intercepts, asymptotes, and sign behavior of the function.
1. If $Q(x)$ has no real zeros, the graph of $P(x)/Q(x)$ is a smooth curve for all real $x$.
2. If $Q(x)$ has real zeros, the graph of $P(x)/Q(x)$ consists of smooth curves on each open interval that does not include a zero. The graph has *vertical asymptotes* at each zero of $Q(x)$.

The line $x = a$ is a vertical asymptote for the graph of a function $f$ if, as $x$ approaches $a$ through values that are greater than or less than $a$, the value of the function grows beyond all bounds, either positive or negative. The cases are shown in the following table, along with the notation generally used:

| Notation | Meaning | Graph |
|---|---|---|
| $\lim\limits_{x \to a^-} f(x) = \infty$ | As $x$ approaches $a$ from the left, $f(x)$ is positive and increases beyond all bounds. | Figure 5-10 |

| Notation | Meaning | Graph |
|---|---|---|
| $\lim\limits_{x \to a^-} f(x) = -\infty$ | As $x$ approaches $a$ from the left, $f(x)$ is negative and decreases beyond all bounds. | 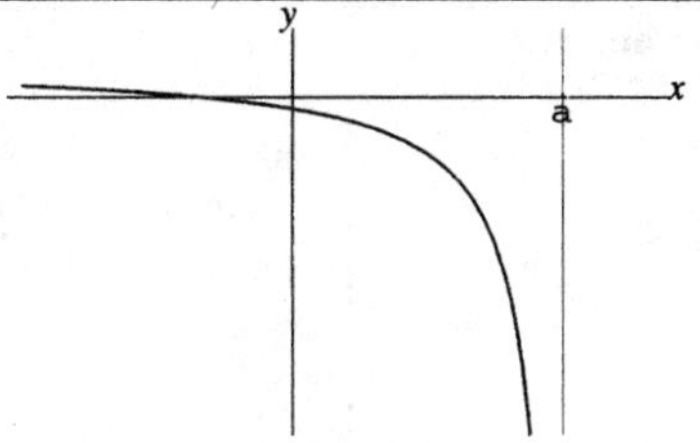 Figure 5-11 |
| $\lim\limits_{x \to a^+} f(x) = \infty$ | As $x$ approaches $a$ from the right, $f(x)$ is positive and increases beyond all bounds. | 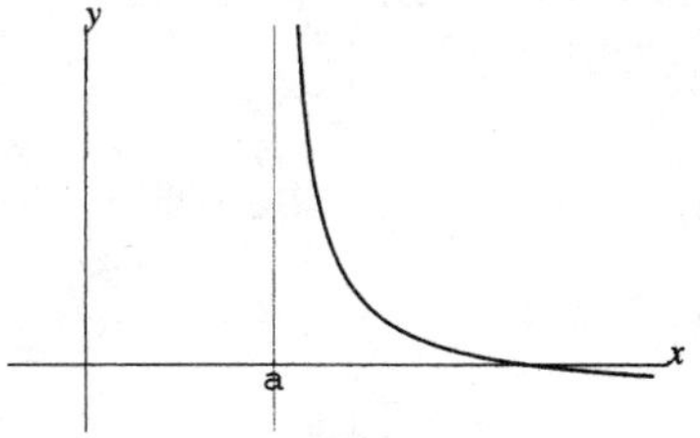 Figure 5-12 |
| $\lim\limits_{x \to a^+} f(x) = -\infty$ | As $x$ approaches $a$ from the right, $f(x)$ is negative and decreases beyond all bounds. | 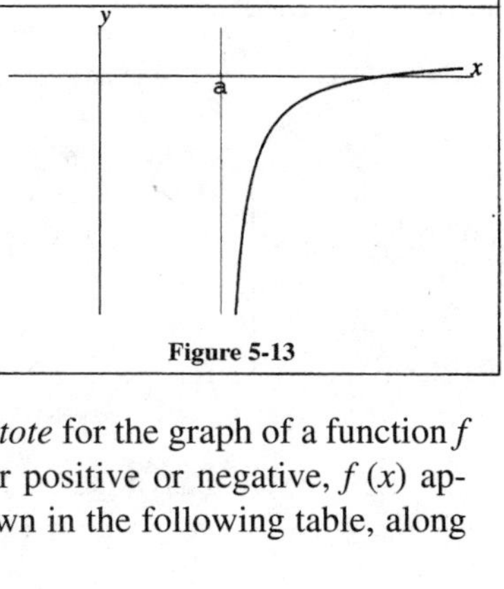 Figure 5-13 |

The line $y = a$ is a *horizontal asymptote* for the graph of a function $f$ if, as $x$ grows beyond all bounds, either positive or negative, $f(x)$ approaches the value $a$. The cases are shown in the following table, along with the notation generally used:

| Notation | Meaning | Graph |
|---|---|---|
| $\lim\limits_{x \to \infty} f(x) = a$ | As $x$ increases beyond all bounds, $f(x)$ approaches the value $a$. [In the figure $f(x) < a$ for large positive values of $x$.] | 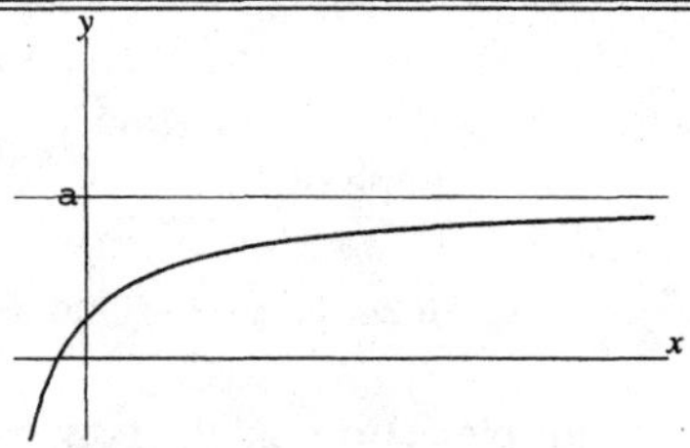 Figure 5-14 |

| Notation | Meaning | Graph |
|---|---|---|
| $\lim\limits_{x \to \infty} f(x) = a$ | As $x$ increases beyond all bounds, $f(x)$ approaches the value $a$. [In the figure $f(x) > a$ for large positive values of $x$.] | 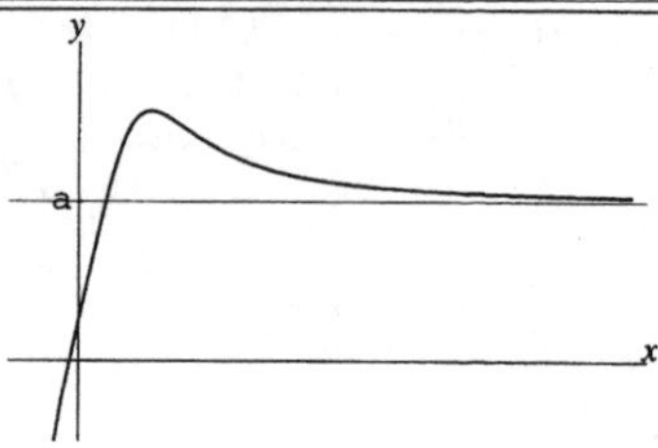 <br>Figure 5-15 |
| $\lim\limits_{x \to -\infty} f(x) = a$ | As $x$ decreases beyond all bounds, $f(x)$ approaches the value $a$. [In the figure $f(x) < a$ for large negative values of $x$.] | 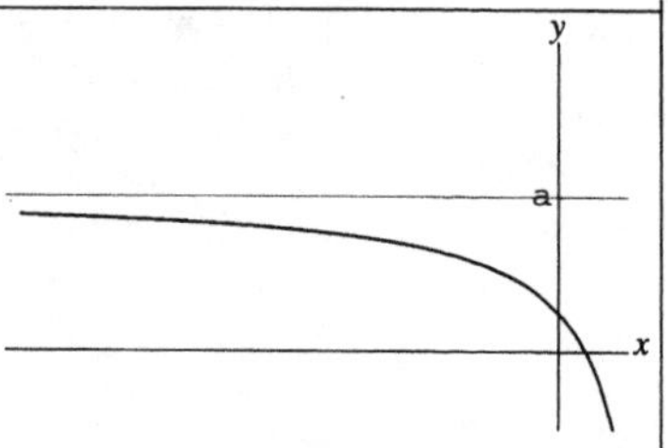 <br>Figure 5-16 |
| $\lim\limits_{x \to -\infty} f(x) = a$ | As $x$ decreases beyond all bounds, $f(x)$ approaches the value $a$. [In the figure $f(x) > a$ for large negative values of $x$.] | 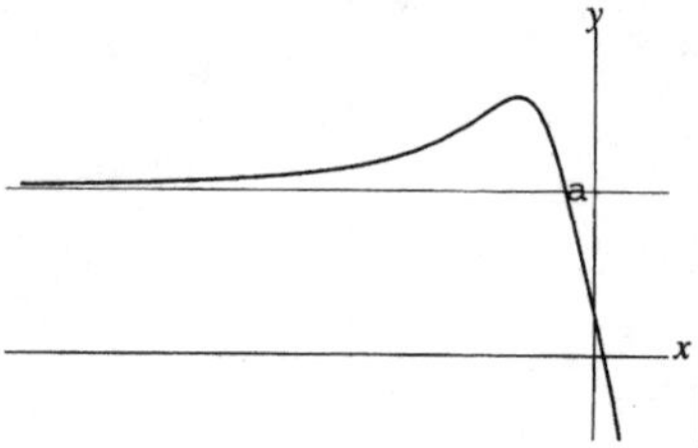 <br>Figure 5-17 |

To find horizontal asymptotes, let

$$f(x) = \frac{P(x)}{Q(x)} = \frac{a_n x^n + \cdots + a_1 x + a_0}{b_m x^m + \cdots + b_1 x + b_0}$$

with $a_n \neq 0$ and $b_m \neq 0$. Then
1. If $n < m$, the $x$-axis is a horizontal asymptote for the graph of $f$.
2. If $n = m$, the line $y = a_n/b_m$ is a horizontal asymptote for the graph of $f$.
3. $n > m$, there is no horizontal asymptote for the graph of $f$. Instead, as $x \to \infty$ and as $x \to -\infty$, either $f(x) \to \infty$ or $f(x) \to -\infty$.

**Example 5.16:** Find the horizontal asymptotes, if any, for $f(x) = \dfrac{2x+1}{x-5}$.

Since the numerator and denominator both have degree 1, the quotient can be written as

$$f(x) = \frac{2x+1}{x} \div \frac{x-5}{x} = \frac{2+\dfrac{1}{x}}{1-\dfrac{5}{x}}$$

For large positive or negative values of $x$, this is very close to $2/1$, the ratio of the leading coefficients, thus $f(x) \to 2$. The line $y = 2$ is a horizontal asymptote.

To find *oblique asymptotes*, let

$$f(x) = \frac{P(x)}{Q(x)} = \frac{a_n x^n + \cdots + a_1 x + a_0}{b_m x^m + \cdots + b_1 x + b_0}$$

with $a_n \neq 0$ and $b_m \neq 0$. Then, if $n = m + 1$, $f(x)$ can be expressed using long division in the form:

$$f(x) = ax + b + \frac{R(x)}{Q(x)}$$

where the degree of $R(x)$ is less than the degree of $Q(x)$. Then, as $x \to \infty$ or $x \to -\infty$, $f(x) \to ax + b$ and the line $y = ax + b$ is an oblique asymptote for the graph of the function.

**Example 5.17:** Find the oblique asymptote for the graph of the function $f(x) = \dfrac{x^3 + 1}{x^2 + x - 2}$.

Use long division to write $f(x) = x - 1 + \dfrac{3x - 1}{x^2 + x - 2}$. Hence, as $x \to \infty$ or $x \to -\infty$, $f(x) \to x - 1$, and the line $y = x - 1$ is an oblique asymptote for the graph of the function.

To sketch the graph of a rational function $y = f(x) = \dfrac{P(x)}{Q(x)}$:

1. Find any $x$-intercepts for the graph [the real zeros of $P(x)$] and plot the corresponding points. Find the $y$-intercept [$f(0)$, assuming $0$ is in the domain of $f$] and plot the point $(0, f(0))$. Analyze the function for any symmetry with respect to the axes or the origin.
2. Find any real zeros of $Q(x)$ and enter any vertical asymptotes for the graph on the sketch.

3. Find any horizontal or oblique asymptote for the graph and enter this on the sketch.
4. Determine whether the graph intersects the horizontal or oblique asymptotes. The graphs of $y = f(x)$ and $y = ax + b$ will intersect at real solutions of $f(x) = ax + b$.
5. Determine, from a sign chart if necessary, the intervals in which the function is positive and negative, then determine the behavior of the function near the asymptotes.
6. Sketch the graph of $f$ in each of the regions found in step 5.

**Example 5.18:** Sketch the graph of the function $f(x) = \dfrac{x+3}{x-2}$.

1. Since $f(0) = -3/2$, the $y$-intercept is $-3/2$. Since $f(x) = 0$ when $x = -3$, the $x$-intercept is $-3$. The graph has no symmetry with respect to the axes or origin.
2. Since $x - 2 = 0$ when $x = 2$, this line is the only vertical asymptote.
3. Since the numerator and denominator both have degree 1, and the ratio of leading coefficients is $1/1$ or 1, the line $y = 1$ is the horizontal asymptote.
4. Since $f(x) = 1$ has no solutions, the graph does not cross its horizontal asymptote.
5. A sign chart shows that the values of the function are positive on $(-\infty, -3)$ and $(2, \infty)$ and negative on $(-3, 2)$. Thus, $\lim\limits_{x \to 2^-} f(x) = -\infty$ and $\lim\limits_{x \to 2^+} f(x) = \infty$. See Figure 5-18.

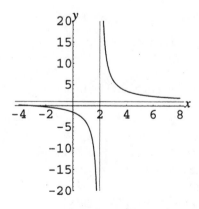

**Figure 5-18**

# Chapter 6
# EXPONENTIAL AND LOGARITHMIC FUNCTIONS

IN THIS CHAPTER

✔ *Exponential Functions*
✔ *Applications of Exponential Functions*
✔ *Logarithmic Functions*
✔ *Applications of Logarithmic Functions*
✔ *Exponential and Logarithmic Equations*
✔ *Solved Problems*

## Exponential Functions

An *exponential function* is any function for which the rule specifies the independent variable is an exponent. A *basic* exponential function has the form $F(x) = a^x$, $a > 0$, $a \neq 1$. The domain of a basic exponential function is considered to be the set of all real numbers, unless otherwise specified.

**Example 6.1:** The following are examples of exponential functions:

(a) $f(x) = 2^x$    (b) $f(x) = \left(\dfrac{1}{2}\right)^x$    (c) $f(x) = 4^{-x}$    (d) $f(x) = 2^{-x^2}$

The properties of exponents can be restated for convenience in terms of variable exponents. Assuming $a, b > 0$, then for all real $x$ and $y$:

$$a^x a^y = a^{x+y} \quad (ab)^x = a^x b^x$$

$$\frac{a^x}{a^y} = a^{x-y} \quad \left(\frac{a}{b}\right)^x = \frac{a^x}{b^x}$$

$$\left(a^P\right)^x = a^{Px}$$

The number $e$ is called the *natural exponential base*. It is defined as $\lim\limits_{n \to \infty}\left(1 + \dfrac{1}{n}\right)^n$. $e$ is an irrational number with a value approximately 2.71828... .

# Applications of Exponential Functions

Applications generally distinguish between exponential *growth* and *decay*. A basic exponential growth function is an increasing exponential function; an exponential decay function is a decreasing exponential function.

**Compound Interest:** If a principal of $P$ dollars is invested at an annual rate of interest $r$, and the interest is compounded $n$ times per year, then the amount of money $A(t)$ generated at time $t$ is given by the formula:

$$A(t) = P\left(1 + \frac{r}{n}\right)^{nt}$$

**Continuous Compound Interest:** If a principal of $P$ dollars is invested at an annual rate of interest $r$, and the interest is compounded continuously, then the amount of money $A(t)$ available at any later time $t$ is given by the formula:

$$A(t) = Pe^{rt}$$

**Unlimited Population Growth:** If a population consisting initially of $N_0$ individuals also is modeled as growing without limit, the population $N(t)$ at any later time $t$ is given by the formula ($k$ is a constant to be determined):

$$N(t) = N_0 e^{kt}$$

Alternatively, a different base can be used.

**Logistic Population Growth:** If a population consisting initially of $N_0$ individuals is modeled as growing with a limiting population (due to limited resources) of $P$ individuals, the population $N(t)$ at any later time $t$ is given by the formula ($k$ is a constant to be determined):

$$N(t) = \frac{N_0 P}{N_0 + (P - N_0)e^{-kt}}$$

**Radioactive Decay:** If an amount $Q_0$ of a radioactive substance is present at time $t = 0$, then the amount $Q(t)$ of the substance present at any later time $t$ is given by the formula ($k$ is a constant to be determined):

$$Q(t) = Q_0 e^{-kt}$$

Alternately, a different base can be used.

## Logarithmic Functions

A logarithmic function, $f(x) = \log_a x$, $a > 0$, $a \neq 1$, is the inverse function to an exponential function $F(x) = a^x$. Thus, if $y = \log_a x$, then $x = a^y$. That is, the logarithm of $x$ to the base $a$ is the exponent to which $a$ must be raised to obtain $x$. Conversely, if $x = a^y$, then $y = \log_a x$. Therefore the relation between logarithmic and exponential functions can be described as:

$$\log_a a^x = x \quad \text{and} \quad a^{\log_a x} = x$$

**Example 6.2:** The function $f(x) = \log_2 x$ is defined as $f: y = \log_2 x$ if $2^y = x$. Since $2^4 = 16$, 4 is the exponent to which 2 must be raised to obtain 16, and $\log_2 16 = 4$.

**Example 6.3:** The statement $10^3 = 1000$ can be rewritten in terms of the logarithm to the base 10. Since 3 is the exponent to which 10 must be raised to obtain 1000, $\log_{10} 1000 = 3$.

**Example 6.4:** $\log_5 125 = \log_5 5^3 = 3$.  $5^{\log_5 25} = 25$

Properties of logarithms: ($M$, $N$ positive real numbers)

$$\log_a 1 = 0 \qquad\qquad \log_a a = 1$$
$$\log_a(MN) = \log_a M + \log_a N \qquad \log_a(M^p) = p \log_a M$$
$$\log_a\left(\frac{M}{N}\right) = \log_a M - \log_a N$$

**Example 6.5:** (*a*) $\log_5 1 = 0$ (since $5^0 = 1$) (*b*) $\log_4 4 = 1$ (since $4^1 = 4$)
(*c*) $\log_6 6x = \log_6 6 + \log_6 x = 1 + \log_6 x$ (*d*) $\log_6 x^6 = 6 \log_6 x$
(*e*) $\log_{1/2}(2x) = \log_{1/2} \dfrac{x}{1/2} = \log_{1/2} x - \log_{1/2}\left(\dfrac{1}{2}\right) = \log_{1/2} x - 1$

There are two special logarithmic functions that have their own abbreviations:
  1.  $\log_{10} x$ is known as the common logarithm and is abbreviated as $\log x$.
  2.  $\log_e x$ is known as the natural logarithm and is abbreviated as $\ln x$.

**Example 6.6:** Write $\dfrac{1}{2}\ln(x+1) - \dfrac{1}{2}\ln(x-1) + \ln C$ as one logarithm.

$$\frac{1}{2}\ln(x+1) - \frac{1}{2}\ln(x-1) + \ln C = \frac{1}{2}[\ln(x+1) - \ln(x-1)] + \ln C$$

$$= \frac{1}{2}\ln\left(\frac{x+1}{x-1}\right) + \ln C$$

$$= \ln\sqrt{\frac{x+1}{x-1}} + \ln C$$

$$= \ln C\sqrt{\frac{x+1}{x-1}}$$

# Applications of Logarithmic Functions

Working with numbers that range over very wide scales, for example, from 0.000000000001 to 10,000,0000,000, can be very cumbersome. The work can be done more efficiently by working with the logarithms of the numbers (as in this example, where the common logarithms range only from $-12$ to $+10$).

Some of examples of logarithmic scales are:

**Sound Intensity:** The decibel scale for measuring sound intensity is defined as follows:

$$D = 10\log\frac{I}{I_0}$$

**Earthquake intensity:** There is more than one logarithmic scale, called a Richter scale, used to measure the destructive power of an earthquake. A commonly used Richter scale is defined as follows:

$$R = \frac{2}{3}\log\frac{E}{E_0}$$

where $R$ is called the (Richter) magnitude of the earthquake, $E$ is the energy released by the earthquake (measured in joules), and $E_0$ is the energy released by a very small reference earthquake.

# Exponential and Logarithmic Equations

*Exponential equations* are equations that involve a variable in an exponent. The crucial step in solving exponential equations is generally to take the logarithm of both sides to an appropriate base, commonly base 10 or base $e$.

**Example 6.7:** Solve $e^x = 2$.

$$e^x = 2 \qquad \text{Take logarithms of both sides}$$
$$\ln(e^x) = \ln(2) \qquad \text{Apply the function - inverse function relation}$$
$$x = \ln 2$$

*Logarithmic equations* are equations that involve the logarithm of a variable or variable expression. The crucial step in solving logarithmic equations is generally to rewrite the logarithmic statement in exponential form. If more than one logarithmic expression is present, these can be combined into one by using properties of logarithms.

**Example 6.8:** Solve $\log_2(x - 3) = 4$

$$\log_2(x-3) = 4 \qquad \text{Rewrite in exponential form}$$
$$2^4 = x - 3 \qquad \text{Isolate the variable}$$
$$x = 2^4 + 3$$
$$x = 19$$

Logarithmic expressions can be rewritten in terms of other bases by means of the change-of-base formula:

$$\log_a x = \frac{\log_b x}{\log_b a}$$

**Example 6.9:** Find an expression, in terms of logarithms to base $e$, for $\log_5 10$, and give an approximate value for the quantity.

From the change-of-base formula, $\log_5 10 = \dfrac{\ln 10}{\ln 5} \approx 1.43$

# Solved Problems

**Solved Problem 6.1:** A certain amount of money $P$ is invested at an annual rate of interest of 4.5%. How many years (to the nearest tenth of a year) would it take for the amount of money to double, assuming interest is compounded quarterly?

Since the money is not compounded continuously use the compound interest formula $A(t) = P\left(1 + \dfrac{r}{n}\right)^{nt}$ with $n = 4$ because it's compounded quarterly and $r = 0.045$ to find $t$ when $A(t) = 2P$.

$$2P = P\left(1 + \frac{0.045}{4}\right)^{4t}$$

$$2 = (1.01125)^{4t}$$

To isolate $t$, take logarithms of both sides to base $e$.

$$\ln 2 = \ln(1.01125)^{4t}$$
$$\ln 2 = 4t \ln(1.01125)$$
$$t = \frac{\ln 2}{4 \ln(1.01125)}$$
$$t \approx 15.5 \text{ years}$$

**Solved Problem 6.2:** In the previous example, how many years (to the nearest tenth of a year) would it take for the amount of money to double, assuming interest is compounded continuously?

Use the formula $A(t) = Pe^{rt}$ with $r = 0.045$, to find $t$ when $A(t) = 2P$.

$$2P = Pe^{0.045t}$$

$$2 = e^{0.045t}$$

To isolate $t$, take logarithms of both sides to base $e$.

$$\ln 2 = \ln e^{0.045t}$$

$$\ln 2 = 0.045t$$

$$t = \frac{\ln 2}{0.045}$$

$$t \approx 15.4 \text{ years}$$

**Solved Problem 6.3:** (a) Find the Richter scale magnitude of an earthquake that releases energy of $1000E_0$. (b) Find energy released by an earthquake that measures 5.0 on the Richter scale, given that $E_0 = 10^{4.40}$ joules.

(a)  Use the formula $R = \frac{2}{3}\log\frac{E}{E_0}$ with $E = 1000E_0$. Then

$$R = \frac{2}{3}\log\frac{1000E_0}{E_0} = \frac{2}{3}\log 1000 = \frac{2}{3}\cdot 3 = 2 \,.$$

(b)  Set $R = 5$. Then $5 = \frac{2}{3}\log\frac{E}{E_0}$. Solving for $E$ yields:

$$\frac{15}{2} = \log\frac{E}{E_0}$$

$$\frac{E}{E_0} = 10^{15/2}$$

$$E = E_0 \cdot 10^{7.5}$$

$$= 10^{4.40} \cdot 10^{7.5}$$

$$= 10^{11.9}$$

$$= 7.94 \times 10^{11} \text{ joules}$$

# Chapter 7
# CONIC SECTIONS

IN THIS CHAPTER

✔ *Loci*
✔ *Parabolas*
✔ *Ellipses*
✔ *Hyperbolas*
✔ *Conic Sections*

## Loci

The set of all points that satisfy specified conditions is called the *locus* (plural: *loci*) of the point under the conditions.

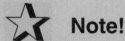 **Note!**

*locus* is the Latin word for place or position.

**Example 7.1:** The locus of a point with positive coordinates is the first quadrant ($x > 0$, $y > 0$).

**Example 7.2:** The locus of points with distance 3 from the origin is the circle $x^2 + y^2 = 9$ with center at $(0, 0)$ and radius 3.

Distance formulas are often used in finding loci.

1. The distance between two points $P_1(x_1,y_1)$ and $P_2(x_2,y_2)$ is given by

$$d(P_1,P_2) = \sqrt{(x_2 - x_1)^2 + (y_2 - y_1)^2}$$

2. The distance from a point $P_1(x_1,y_1)$ to a straight line $Ax + By + C = 0$ is given by:

$$d = \frac{|Ax_1 + By_1 + C|}{\sqrt{A^2 + B^2}}$$

**Example 7.3:** Find the locus of points $P(x,y)$ equidistant from $P_1(1,0)$ and $P_2(3,0)$.

Set $d(P,P_1) = d(P, P_2)$. Then

$$\sqrt{(x-1)^2 + (y-0)^2} = \sqrt{(x-3)^2 + (y-0)^2} .$$

Simplifying yields:

$$(x-1)^2 + (y-0)^2 = (x-3)^2 + (y-0)^2$$
$$x^2 - 2x + 1 + y^2 = x^2 - 6x + 9 + y^2$$
$$4x = 8$$
$$x = 2$$

The locus is a vertical line that forms the perpendicular bisector of $P_1P_2$.

# Parabolas

A *parabola* is defined as the locus of points $P$ equidistant from a given point and a given line, that is, $PF = PD$, where $F$ is the given point, called the *focus*, and $PD$ is the distance to the given line $l$, called the *directrix*. A line through the focus perpendicular to the directrix is called the *axis* (or *axis of symmetry*) and the point on the axis halfway between the directrix and the focus is called the *vertex*.

A parabola with axis parallel to one of the coordinate axes is said to be in *standard orientation*. If, in addition, the vertex of the parabola is at the origin, the parabola is said to be in one of four *standard positions*: opening right, opening left, opening up, and opening down.

Graphs of parabolas in standard positions with their equations and characteristics are shown in Figures 7-1 to 7-4.

| Opening Right | Opening Left |
|---|---|
| Vertex: (0,0)<br>Focus: $F(p,0)$<br>Directrix: $x = -p$ | Vertex: (0,0)<br>Focus: $F(-p,0)$<br>Directrix: $x = p$ |
| Equation:<br>$y^2 = 4px$ | Equation:<br>$y^2 = -4px$ |
| 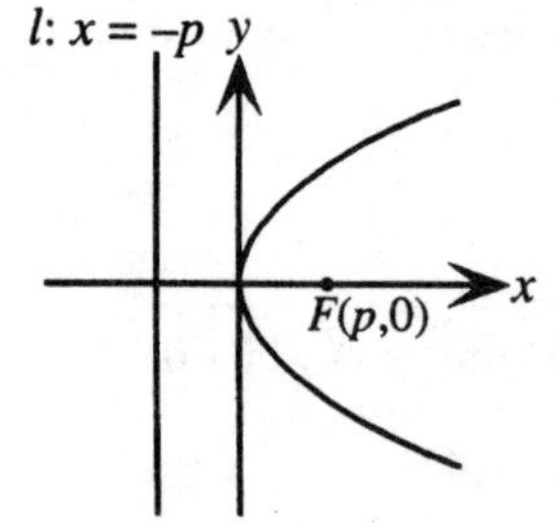 Figure 7-1 | 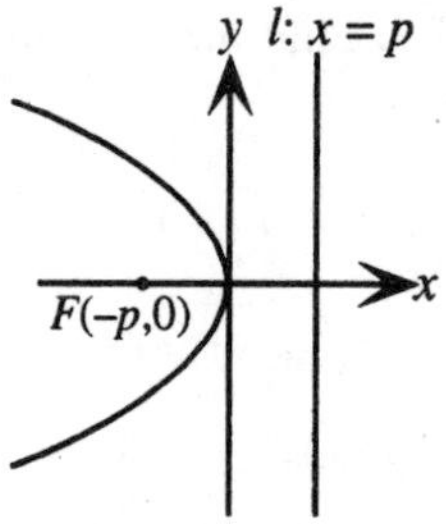 Figure 7-2 |

| Opening Up | Opening Down |
|---|---|
| Vertex: (0,0)<br>Focus: $F(0,p)$<br>Directrix: $y = -p$ | Vertex: (0,0)<br>Focus: $F(0,-p)$<br>Directrix: $y = p$ |
| Equation:<br>$x^2 = 4py$ | Equation:<br>$x^2 = -4py$ |
| 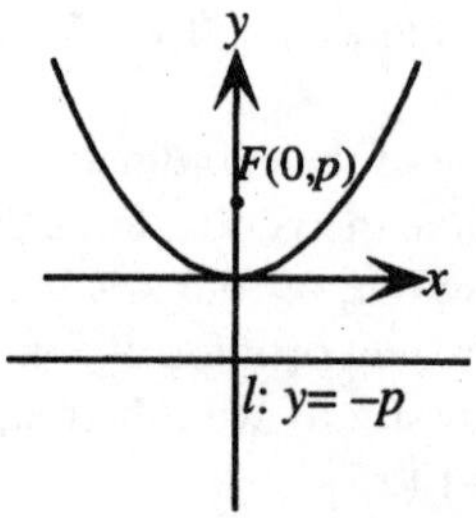 Figure 7-3 | 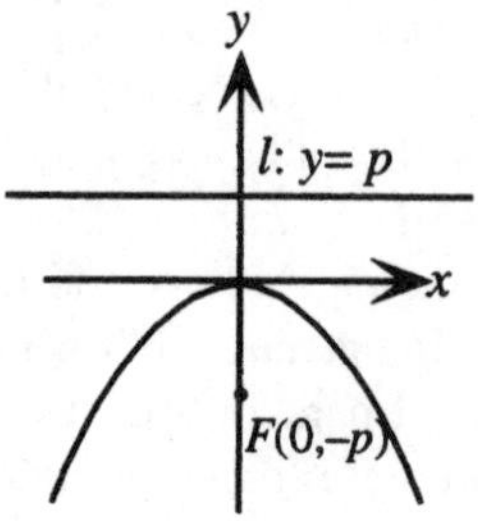 Figure 7-4 |

Replacing $x$ by $x - h$ has the effect of shifting the graph of an equation by $|h|$ units, to the right if $h$ is positive, to the left if $h$ is negative. Similarly, replacing $y$ by $y - k$ has the effect of shifting the graph by $|k|$ units, up if $k$ is positive and down if $k$ is negative. The equations and characteristics of parabolas in standard orientation, but not necessarily in standard position, are shown in the following table.

| **Opening Right** | **Opening Left** |
|---|---|
| Equation $(y-k)^2 = 4p(x-h)$ | Equation $(y-k)^2 = -4p(x-h)$ |
| Vertex: $(h,k)$ <br> Focus: $F(h + p,k)$ <br> Directrix: <br> $x = h - p$ | Vertex: $(h,k)$ <br> Focus: $F(h - p,k)$ <br> Directrix: <br> $x = h + p$ |

| **Opening Up** | **Opening Down** |
|---|---|
| Equation: $(x - h)^2 = 4p(y-k)$ | Equation: $(x - h)^2 = -4p(y-k)$ |
| Vertex: $(h,k)$ <br> Focus: $F(h,k + p)$ <br> Directrix: <br> $y = k - p$ | Vertex: $(h,k)$ <br> Focus: $F(h,k - p)$ <br> Directrix: <br> $y = k + p$ |

**Example 7.4:** Show that $y^2 - 8x + 2y + 9 = 0$ is the equation of a parabola. Find the focus, directrix, vertex, and axis, and sketch a graph.

Complete the square on $y$ to obtain:

$$y^2 + 2y = 8x - 9$$
$$y^2 + 2y + 1 = 8x - 8$$
$$(y + 1)^2 = 8(x - 1)$$

Thus $p = 2$, $h = 1$, and $k = -1$. Hence the parabola is in standard orientation, with vertex $(1, -1)$, opening right, and thus has focus at $(h + p, k) = (2 + 1, -1) = (3, -1)$. The directrix of the parabola is the line $x = h - p = 1 - 2 = -1$ and the axis is the line $y = -1$. The graph is shown in Figure 7-5.

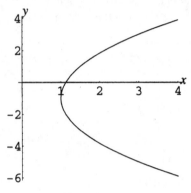

**Figure 7-5**

# Ellipses

The locus of points $P$ such that the sum of the distances from $P$ to two fixed points is constant is called an *ellipse*. Thus, let $F_1$ and $F_2$ be the two points (called *foci*, the plural of *focus*), then the defining relation for the ellipse is $PF_1 + PF_2 = 2a$. The line through the foci is called the *focal axis* of the ellipse; the point on the focal axis halfway between the foci is called the *center*; the points where the ellipse crosses the focal axis are called the *vertices*. The line segment joining the two vertices is called the *major axis*, and the line segment through the center, perpendicular to the major axis, with both endpoints on the ellipse, is called the *minor axis*. (See Figure 7-6.)

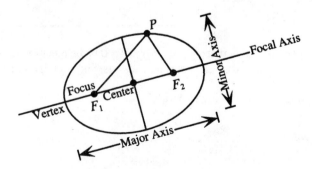

**Figure 7-6**

An ellipse with focal axis parallel to one of the coordinate axes is said to be in *standard orientation*. If, in addition, the center of the ellipse is at the origin, the ellipse is said to be in one of two *standard positions*: with foci on the $x$-axis or with foci on the $y$-axis.

Graphs of ellipses in standard position with their equations and characteristics are shown in the following table:

| Foci on $x$-axis | Foci on $y$-axis |
|---|---|
| Equation: $\dfrac{x^2}{a^2} + \dfrac{y^2}{b^2} = 1$ <br> where $b^2 = a^2 - c2$ <br> Note: $a > b, a > c$ | Equation: $\dfrac{x^2}{b^2} + \dfrac{y^2}{a^2} = 1$ <br> where $b^2 = a^2 - c^2$ <br> Note: $a > b, a > c$ |
| Foci: $F_1(-c, 0), F_2(c, 0)$ <br> Vertices: $(-a, 0), (a, 0)$ <br> Center: $(0, 0)$ | Foci: $F_1(0, -c), F_2(0, c)$ <br> Vertices: $(0, -a), (0, a)$ <br> Center: $(0, 0)$ |
| <br> **Figure 7-7** | <br> **Figure 7-8** |

**Example 7.5:** Analyze and sketch the graph of $4x^2 + 9y^2 = 36$.

Written in standard form the equation becomes

$$\frac{x^2}{9} + \frac{y^2}{4} = 1$$

Thus $a = 3$ and $b = 2$. Therefore $c = \sqrt{a^2 - b^2} = \sqrt{9-4} = \sqrt{5}$. Hence the ellipse is in standard position with foci at $\left(\pm\sqrt{5}, 0\right)$, $x$-intercepts $(\pm 3, 0)$ and $y$-intercepts $(0, \pm 2)$. The graph is shown in Figure 7-9.

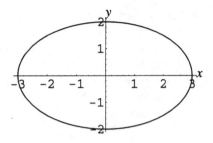

**Figure 7-9**

# Hyperbolas

The locus of points $P$ such that the absolute value of the difference of the distances from $P$ to two fixed points is a constant is called a *hyperbola*. Thus, let $F_1$ and $F_2$ be the two points (*foci*), then the defining relation for the hyperbola is $|PF_1 - PF_2| = 2a$. The line through the foci is called the *focal axis* of the hyperbola; the point on the focal axis halfway between the foci is called the *center*; the points where the hyperbola crosses the focal axis are called the *vertices*. The line segment joining the two vertices is called the *transverse axis*. (See Figure 7-10.)

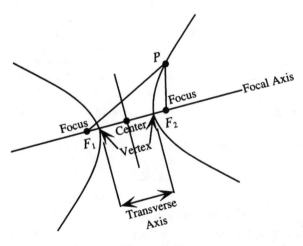

**Figure 7-10**

A hyperbola with focal axis parallel to one of the coordinate axes is said to be in *standard orientation*. If, in addition, the center of the hyperbola is at the origin, the hyperbola is said to be in one of two *standard positions*: with foci on the $x$-axis (Figure 7-11) or with foci on the $y$-axis (Figure 7-12).

Graphs of hyperbolas in standard position with their equations and characteristics are shown in the following table:

| Foci on *x*-axis | Foci on *y*-axis |
|---|---|
| Foci: $F_1(-c,0)$, $F_2(c,0)$<br>Vertices: $(-a,0)$, $(a,0)$<br>Center: $(0,0)$ | Foci: $F_1(0,-c)$, $F_2(0,c)$<br>Vertices: $(0,-a)$, $(0,a)$<br>Center: $(0,0)$ |
| Equation: $\dfrac{x^2}{a^2} - \dfrac{y^2}{b^2} = 1$<br>where $b^2 = c^2 - a^2$<br>Note: $c > a,\ c > b$ | Equation: $\dfrac{y^2}{a^2} - \dfrac{x^2}{b^2} = 1$<br>where $b^2 = c^2 - a^2$<br>Note: $c > a,\ c > b$ |
| Asymptotes: $y = \pm \dfrac{b}{a} x$ | Asymptotes: $y = \pm \dfrac{a}{b} x$ |
| Asymptote / Vertex / Vertex / Focus / Focus / Asymptote<br>**Figure 7-11** | Focus / Asymptote / Vertex / Asymptote / Vertex / Focus<br>**Figure 7-12** |

A measure of the shape for an ellipse or hyperbola is the quantity $e = \dfrac{c}{a}$, called the *eccentricity*. For an ellipse, $0 < e < 1$; for a hyperbola $e > 1$.

# Conic Sections

The curves that result from the intersection of a plane with a cone are called *conic sections*. Figure 7-13 shows the four major possibilities: circle, ellipse, parabola, and hyperbola.

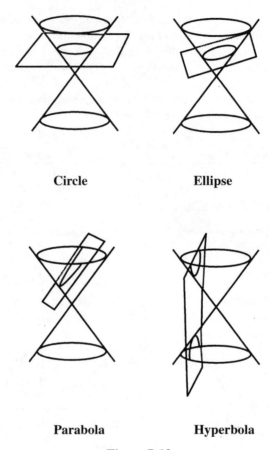

**Circle**          **Ellipse**

**Parabola**          **Hyperbola**

**Figure 7-13**

The graph of a second-degree equation in two variables $Ax^2 + Bxy + Cy^2 + Dx + Ey + F = 0$ is a *conic section*. Ignoring degenerate cases, the possibilities are as follows:

   A.   If no $xy$ term is present ($B = 0$):
- If $A = C$ the graph is a circle. Otherwise $A \neq C$; then:
- If $AC = 0$ the graph is a parabola.
- If $AC > 0$ the graph is an ellipse.
- If $AC < 0$ the graph is a hyperbola.

   B.   In general:
- If $B^2 - 4AC = 0$ the graph is a parabola.
- If $B^2 - 4AC < 0$ the graph is an ellipse.
- If $B^2 - 4AC > 0$ the graph is a hyperbola.

# Chapter 8
# TRIGONOMETRIC FUNCTIONS

IN THIS CHAPTER

✔ *Unit Circle*
✔ *Trigonometric Functions*
✔ *Trigonometric Identities*
✔ *Graphs of Sine and Cosine Functions*
✔ *Graphs of the Other Trigonometric Functions*
✔ *Angles*

## Unit Circle

The *unit circle* is the circle $U$ with center $(0,0)$ and radius 1. The equation of the unit circle is $x^2 + y^2 = 1$. The circumference of the unit circle is $2\pi$.

**Example 8.1:** Draw a unit circle (see Figure 8-1) and indicate its intercepts.

87

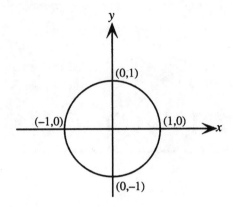

**Figure 8-1**

A unique point $P$ on a unit circle $U$ can be associated with any given real number $t$ in the following manner:

1. Associated with $t = 0$ is the point $(1,0)$.
2. Associated with any *positive* real number $t$ is the point $P(x,y)$ found by proceeding a distance $t$ along the circle in the *counterclockwise* direction from the point $(1,0)$ (see Figure 8-2).
3. Associated with any *negative* real number $t$ is the point $P(x,y)$ found by proceeding a distance $|t|$ along the circle in the *clockwise* direction from the point $(1,0)$ (see Figure 8-3).

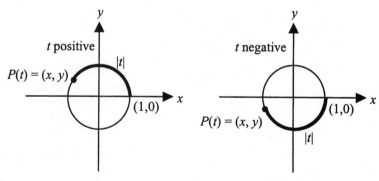

**Figure 8-2**                    **Figure 8-3**

**Example 8.2:** Find (a) $P(0)$, (b) $P(\pi)$ , (c) $P(\pi/2)$, (d) $P(-\pi/2)$, and (e) $P(\pi/4)$. (See Figure 8-4.)

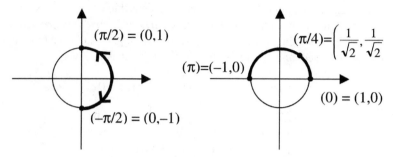

**Fig. 8-4**

1. By the first rule given above, $P(0) = (1,0)$.
2. Since $\pi$ is half of the circumference of the unit circle, $P(\pi)$ is half of the way around the unit circle in the counterclockwise direction from $(1,0)$; that is, $P(\pi) = (-1,0)$.
3. Since $\pi/2$ is a quarter of the circumference of the unit circle, $P(\pi/2)$ is a quarter of the way around the unit circle in the counterclockwise direction from $(1,0)$; that is, $P(\pi/2) = (0,1)$.

4. $P(-\pi/2)$ is a quarter of the way around the unit circle in the clockwise direction from $(1,0)$; that is, $P(\pi/2) = (0,-1)$.
5. Since $\pi/4$ is one-half the way from 0 to $\pi/2$, the point $P(\pi/4) = (x,y)$ lies on the line $y = x$. Thus coordinates $(x,y)$ satisfy both the equations $x^2 + y^2 = 1$ and $y = x$. Substituting yields:

$$x^2 + x^2 = 1$$
$$2x^2 = 1$$
$$x^2 = \frac{1}{2}$$
$$x = \frac{1}{\sqrt{2}} = \frac{\sqrt{2}}{2} \text{ (since } x \text{ is positive)}$$

For any real number $t$ the following relations can be shown to hold:
1. $P(t + 2\pi) = P(t)$.
2. If $P(t) = (x,y)$, then $P(-t) = (x,-y)$.
3. If $P(t) = (x,y)$, then $P(t + \pi) = (-x,-y)$.

# Trigonometric Functions

If $t$ is a real number and $P(x,y)$ is the point, referred to as $P(t)$, on the unit circle $U$ that corresponds to $P$, then the six *trigonometric functions* of $t$, sine, cosine, tangent, cosecant, secant, and cotangent, abbreviated sin, cos, tan, csc, sec, and cot, respectively, are defined as follows:

$$\sin t = y \qquad\qquad \csc t = \frac{1}{y} \ (\text{if } y \neq 0)$$

$$\cos t = x \qquad\qquad \sec t = \frac{1}{x} \ (\text{if } x \neq 0)$$

$$\tan t = \frac{y}{x} \ (\text{if } x \neq 0) \quad \cot t = \frac{x}{y} (\text{if } y \neq 0)$$

**Example 8.3:** If $t$ is a real number such that $P\left(\frac{3}{5}, -\frac{4}{5}\right)$ is the point on the unit circle that corresponds to $t$, find the six trigonometric functions of $t$.

Since the $x$-coordinate of $P$ is 3/5 and the $y$-coordinate of $P$ is $-4/5$, the six trigonometric functions of $t$ are as follows:

$$\sin t = y = -\frac{4}{5} \qquad \cos t = x = \frac{3}{5} \qquad \tan t = \frac{y}{x} = \frac{-4/5}{3/5} = -\frac{4}{3}$$

$$\csc t = \frac{1}{y} = \frac{1}{-4/5} = -\frac{5}{4} \quad \sec t = \frac{1}{x} = \frac{1}{3/5} = \frac{5}{3} \quad \cot t = \frac{x}{y} = \frac{3/5}{-4/5} = -\frac{3}{4}$$

**Example 8.4:** Determine the signs of the six trigonometric functions of $P(t) = (x,y)$ in each of the four quadrants.

1.  In quadrant I, both $x$ and $y$ are positive. Therefore all trigonometric functions are positive in quadrant I
2.  In quadrant II, the $x$ value is negative and the $y$ value is positive. Therefore only sin $t$ and csc $t$ are positive while the other trigonometric functions are negative.
3.  In quadrant III, both $x$ and $y$ are negative. Therefore only tan $t$ and cot $t$ are positive while the other trigonometric functions are negative.
4.  In quadrant IV, the $x$ value is positive and the $y$ value is negative. Therefore only cos $t$ and sec $t$ are positive while the other trigonometric functions are negative.

A function $f$ is called *periodic* if there exists a real number $p$ such that $f(t + p) = f(t)$ for every real number $t$ in the domain of $f$. The smallest such real number is called the *period* of the function.

The trigonometric functions are all periodic. The following important relations can be shown to hold:

$$\sin(t + 2\pi) = \sin t \quad \cos(t + 2\pi) = \cos t \quad \tan(t + \pi) = \tan t$$
$$\csc(t + 2\pi) = \csc t \quad \sec(t + 2\pi) = \sec t \quad \cot(t + \pi) = \cot t$$

The expressions for the squares of the trigonometric functions arise frequently. $(\sin t)^2$ is generally written $\sin^2 t$, $(\cos t)^2$ is generally written $\cos^2 t$, and so on. Similarly, $(\sin t)^3$ is generally written $\sin^3 t$, and so on.

## Trigonometric Identities

An *identity* is an equation that is true for all values of the variables it contains, as long as both sides are meaningful.

There are several important trigonometric identities:

1. *Pythagorean Identities.* For all $t$ for which both sides are defined:

$$\cos^2 t + \sin^2 t = 1 \quad 1 + \tan^2 t = \sec^2 t \quad \cot^2 t + 1 = \csc^2 t$$

2. *Reciprocal Identities.* For all $t$ for which both sides are defined:

$$\csc t = \frac{1}{\sin t} \quad \sec t = \frac{1}{\cos t} \quad \cot t = \frac{1}{\tan t}$$

3. *Quotient Identities.* For all $t$ for which both sides are defined:

$$\tan t = \frac{\sin t}{\cos t} \qquad \cot t = \frac{\cos t}{\sin t}$$

4. *Identities for Negatives.* For all $t$ for which both sides are defined:

$$\sin(-t) = -\sin t \quad \cos(-t) = \cos t \quad \tan(-t) = -\tan t$$
$$\csc(-t) = -\csc t \quad \sec(-t) = \sec t \quad \cot(-t) = -\cot t$$

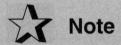 **Note**

Since $\cos^2 t + \sin^2 t = 1$, it is also true that
$\cos^2 t = 1 - \sin^2 t$ and $\sin^2 t = 1 - \cos^2 t$.
The same holds true for the other identities as well.

# Graphs of Sine and Cosine Functions

The domains of $f(t) = \sin t$ and $f(t) = \cos t$ are identical: all real numbers, $R$. The ranges of these functions are also identical: the interval $[-1, 1]$. The graph of $u = \sin t$ is shown in Figure 8-5.

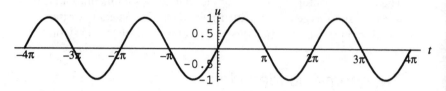

**Figure 8-5**

The graph of $u = \cos t$ is shown in Figure 8-6.

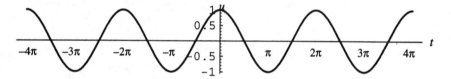

**Figure 8-6**

The function $f(t) = \sin t$ is periodic with period $2\pi$. Its graph repeats a *cycle*, regarded as the portion of the graph for $0 \leq t \leq 2\pi$. The graph is often referred to as the *basic sine curve*. The *amplitude* of the basic sine curve, defined as half the difference between the maximum and minimum values of the function, is 1. The function $f(t) = \cos t$ is also periodic with period $2\pi$. Its graph, called the *basic cosine curve*, also repeats a cycle, regarded as the portion of this graph for $0 \leq t \leq 2\pi$. The graph can also be thought of as a sine curve with amplitude 1, shifted left by an amount $\pi/2$.

The graphs of other sine and cosine functions can be obtained by using the transformations described in Chapter 4. The graphs of the transformations of the sine function are described but the same descriptions may be applied to transformations of the other trigonometric functions as well.

1. Graph of $u = A \sin t$. The graph of $u = A \sin t$ for positive $A$ is a basic sine curve, but stretched by a factor of $A$, hence with amplitude $A$, referred to as a *standard* sine curve. The graph of $u =$

A sin $t$ for negative $A$ is a standard sine curve with amplitude $|A|$, reflected with respect to the vertical axis, called an *upside-down sine curve*.

2. Graph of $u = \sin bt$ ($b$ positive). The graph of $u = \sin bt$ is a standard sine curve, compressed by a factor of $b$ with respect to the $x$-axis, hence with period $2\pi/b$.

3. Graph of $u = \sin(t - c)$. The graph of $u = \sin(t - c)$ is a standard sine curve shifted to the right $|c|$ units if $c$ is positive, shifted to the left $|c|$ units if $c$ is negative. $c$ is referred to as the *phase shift*.

4. Graph of $u = \sin t + d$. The graph of $u = \sin t + d$ is a standard sine curve shifted up $|d|$ units if $d$ is positive, shifted down $|d|$ units if $d$ is negative.

5. Graph of $u = A \sin(bt - c) + d$ displays combinations of the above features. In general, assuming $A$, $b$, $c$, $d$ positive, the graph is a standard sine curve with amplitude $A$, period $2\pi/b$, phase shift $c/b$, shifted up $d$ units.

**Example 8.5:** Sketch $u = -\dfrac{1}{2}\cos\left(3t + \dfrac{\pi}{4}\right) + \dfrac{3}{2}$.

The graph (Figure 8-7) is an upside-down cosine curve with amplitude 1/2, period $2\pi/3$ and phase shift $(-\pi/4) \div 3 = -\pi/12$. Divide the interval from $-\pi/12$ to $7\pi/12$ (= phase shift + one period) into four equal subintervals and sketch the curve with maximum height 2 and minimum height 1.

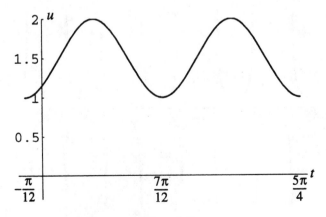

**Figure 8-7**

# Graphs of the Other Trigonometric Functions

1.  *Tangent*. The domain of the tangent function is $\{t \in \mathbf{R} \mid t \neq \pi/2 + 2\pi n,\ 3\pi/2 + 2\pi n\ \}$, and the range is $\mathbf{R}$. The graph is shown in Figure 8-8.

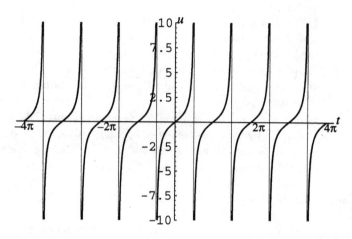

**Figure 8-8**

2.  *Secant*. The domain of the secant function is $\{t \in \mathbf{R} \mid t \neq \pi/2 + 2\pi n,\ 3\pi/2 + 2\pi n\ \}$ and the range is $(-\infty, -1] \cup [1, \infty)$. The graph is shown in Figure 8-9.

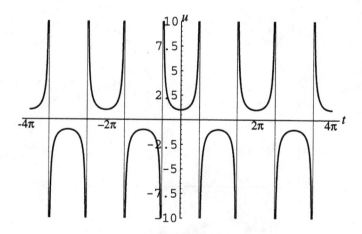

**Figure 8-9**

3. *Cotangent.* The domain of the cotangent function is $\{t \in \mathbf{R} \mid t \neq n\pi\}$ and the range is $\mathbf{R}$. The graph is shown below in Figure 8-10.

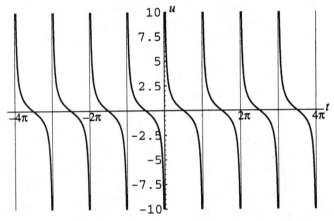

**Figure 8-10**

4. *Cosecant.* The domain of the cosecant function is $\{t \in \mathbf{R} \mid t \neq n\pi\}$ and the range is $(-\infty, -1] \cup [1, \infty)$. The graph is shown below in Figure 8-11.

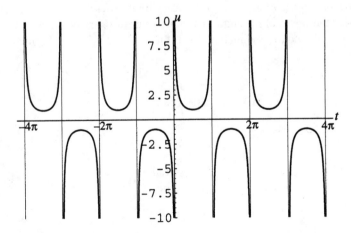

**Figure 8-11**

**Example 8.6:** Sketch a graph of $u = \tan(t - \pi/3)$.

The graph is the same as the graph of $u = \tan t$ shifted $\pi/3$ units to the right, and has period $\pi$. Since $\tan T$ goes through one cycle in the interval $-\pi/2 < T < \pi/2$, $\tan(t - \pi/3)$ goes through one cycle in the interval $-\pi/2 < t - \pi/3 < \pi/2$, that is, $-\pi/6 < t < 5\pi/6$. Sketch the graph in this interval and repeat the cycle with period $\pi$. (See Figure 8-12.)

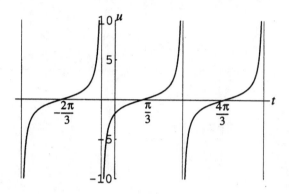

**Figure 8-12**

## Angles

A *trigonometric angle* is determined by rotating a ray about its endpoint, called the *vertex* of the angle. The starting position of the ray is called the *initial side* and the ending position is the *terminal side*. (See Figure 8-13.)

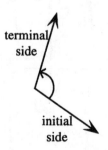

**Figure 8-13**

If the displacement of the ray from its starting position is in the counterclockwise direction, the angle is assigned a positive measure, if in the clockwise direction, a negative measure. A zero angle corresponds to zero displacement; the initial and terminal sides of a zero angle are coincident.

An angle is in *standard position* in a Cartesian coordinate system if its vertex is at the origin and its initial side is the positive *x*-axis. Angles in standard position are categorized by their terminal sides: If the terminal side falls along an axis, the angle is called a *quadrantal angle;* if the terminal side is in quadrant *n*, the angle is referred to as a *quadrant n angle*.

In calculus, angles are normally measured in radian measure. One radian is defined as the measure of an angle that, if placed with vertex at the center of a circle, subtends (intersects) an arc of length equal to the radius of the circle. In Figure 8-14, angle $\theta$ has measure 1 radian.

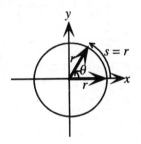

**Figure 8-14**

Since the circumference of a circle of radius *r* has length $2\pi r$, a positive angle of one full revolution corresponds to an arc length of $2\pi r$ and thus has measure $2\pi$ radians. (See Figure 8-15).

**Example 8.7:** Draw examples of angles of measures $\pi$, and $\dfrac{\pi}{2}$ .

| Measure $\pi$ | Measure $\pi/2$ |
|:---:|:---:|
| | |

**Figure 8-15**

In applications, angles are commonly measured in degrees (°). A positive angle of one full revolution has a measure of 360°. Thus $2\pi$ radians $= 360°$, or $180° = \pi$ radians.

To transform radian measure into degrees, use this relation in the form $180°/\pi = 1$ radian and multiply the radian measure by $180°/\pi$. To transform degree measure into radians, use the relation in the form $1° = \pi/180$ radians and multiply the degree measure by $\pi/180°$. The following table summarizes the measures of common angles:

| Degrees | 0° | 30° | 45° | 60° | 90° | 120° | 180° | 270° | 360° |
|---|---|---|---|---|---|---|---|---|---|
| Radians | 0 | $\dfrac{\pi}{6}$ | $\dfrac{\pi}{4}$ | $\dfrac{\pi}{3}$ | $\dfrac{\pi}{2}$ | $\dfrac{2\pi}{3}$ | $\pi$ | $\dfrac{3\pi}{2}$ | $2\pi$ |

**Example 8.8:** (*a*) Transform 210° into radians. (*b*) Transform $6\pi$ radians into degrees.

(*a*) $\quad 210° = 210° \cdot \dfrac{\pi}{180°} = \dfrac{7\pi}{6}$ radians;

(*b*) $\quad 6\pi$ radians $= 6\pi \cdot \dfrac{180°}{\pi} = 1080°$

An angle of measure between 0 and $\pi/2$ radians (between 0° and 90°) is called an *acute* angle. An angle of measure $\pi/2$ radians (90°) is called a *right* angle. An angle of measure between $\pi/2$ and $\pi$ radians (between 90° and 180°) is called an *obtuse* angle. An angle of measure $\pi$ radians (180°) is called a *straight* angle.

# You Need to Know

An angle is normally referred to by giving its measure; thus $\theta = 30°$ means that $\theta$ has a measure of 30°.

If $\alpha$ and $\beta$ are two angles such that $\alpha + \beta = \pi/2$, $\alpha$ and $\beta$ are called *complementary* angles. If $\alpha$ and $\beta$ are two angles such that $\alpha + \beta = \pi$, $\alpha$ and $\beta$ are called *supplementary* angles.

**Example 8.9:** Find an angle complementary to $\theta$ if
(*a*) $\theta = \pi/3$; (*b*) $\theta = 37.25°$

(a) The complementary angle to $\theta$ is $\pi/2 - \theta = \pi/2 - \pi/3 = \pi/6$.
(b) The complementary angle to $\theta$ is $90° - \theta = 90° - 37.25°$ $= 52.75°$.

Two angles in standard position are coterminal if they have the same terminal side. There are an infinite number of angles coterminal with a given angle. To find an angle coterminal with a given angle, add or subtract $2\pi$ (if the angle is measured in radians) or $360°$ (if the angle is measured in degrees).

**Example 8.10:** Find two angles that are coterminal with
(a) 2 radians; (b) −60°.

(a) Coterminal with 2 radians are $2 + 2\pi$ and $2 - 2\pi$ radians as well as many other angles.
(b) Coterminal with $-60°$ are $-60° + 360° = 300°$ and $-60° - 360°$ $= -420°$, as well as many other angles.

Let $\theta$ be an angle in standard position, and $P(x,y)$ be any point except the origin on the terminal side of $\theta$. If $r = \sqrt{x^2 + y^2}$ is the distance from $P$ to the origin, then the six trigonometric functions of $\theta$ are given by:

$$\sin\theta = \frac{y}{r} \qquad \cos\theta = \frac{x}{r} \qquad \tan\theta = \frac{y}{x} \text{ (if } x \neq 0)$$

$$\csc\theta = \frac{r}{y} \text{ (if } y \neq 0) \quad \sec\theta = \frac{r}{x} \text{ (if } x \neq 0) \quad \cot\theta = \frac{x}{y} \text{ (if } y \neq 0)$$

**Example 8.11:** Let $\theta$ be an angle in standard position with $P(-3,4)$ a point on the terminal side of $\theta$ (see Figure 8-16).

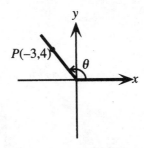

**Figure 8-16**

$x = -3$, $y = 4$, $r = \sqrt{x^2 + y^2} = \sqrt{(-3)^2 + (4)^2} = 5$; hence

$$\sin\theta = \frac{y}{r} = \frac{4}{5} \quad \cos\theta = \frac{x}{r} = -\frac{3}{5} \quad \tan\theta = \frac{y}{x} = -\frac{4}{3}$$

$$\csc\theta = \frac{r}{y} = \frac{5}{4} \quad \sec\theta = \frac{r}{x} = -\frac{5}{3} \quad \cot\theta = \frac{x}{y} = -\frac{3}{4}$$

If $\theta$ is an acute angle, it can be regarded as an angle of a right triangle. Placing $\theta$ in standard position, and naming the sides of the right triangle as hypotenuse (hyp), opposite (opp), and adjacent (adj), the lengths of the adjacent and opposite sides are the $x$- and $y$-coordinates, respectively, of a point on the terminal side of the angle. The length of the hypotenuse is $r = \sqrt{x^2 + y^2}$.

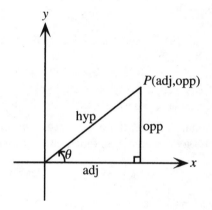

**Figure 8-17**

For an acute angle $\theta$, the trigonometric functions of $\theta$ are then as follows:

$$\sin\theta = \frac{y}{r} = \frac{\text{opp}}{\text{hyp}} \quad \cos\theta = \frac{x}{r} = \frac{\text{adj}}{\text{hyp}} \quad \tan\theta = \frac{y}{x} = \frac{\text{opp}}{\text{adj}}$$

$$\csc\theta = \frac{r}{y} = \frac{\text{hyp}}{\text{opp}} \quad \sec\theta = \frac{r}{x} = \frac{\text{hyp}}{\text{adj}} \quad \cot\theta = \frac{x}{y} = \frac{\text{adj}}{\text{opp}}$$

**Example 8.12:** Find the six trigonometric functions of $\theta$ as shown in Figure 8-18.

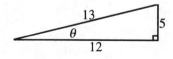

**Figure 8-18**

For $\theta$ as shown, opp = 5, adj = 12, hyp = 13, hence

$$\sin\theta = \frac{\text{opp}}{\text{hyp}} = \frac{5}{13} \qquad \cos\theta = \frac{\text{adj}}{\text{hyp}} = \frac{12}{13} \qquad \tan\theta = \frac{\text{opp}}{\text{adj}} = \frac{5}{12}$$

$$\csc\theta = \frac{\text{hyp}}{\text{opp}} = \frac{13}{5} \qquad \sec\theta = \frac{\text{hyp}}{\text{adj}} = \frac{13}{12} \qquad \cot\theta = \frac{\text{adj}}{\text{opp}} = \frac{12}{5}$$

The reference angle for $\theta$, a nonquadrantal angle in standard position, is the acute angle $\theta_R$ between the x-axis and the terminal side of $\theta$. Figure 8-19 shows angles and reference angles for cases $0 < \theta < 2\pi$. To find reference angles for other nonquadrantal angles, first add or subtract multiples of $2\pi$ to obtain an angle coterminal with $\theta$ that satisfies $0 < \theta < 2\pi$.

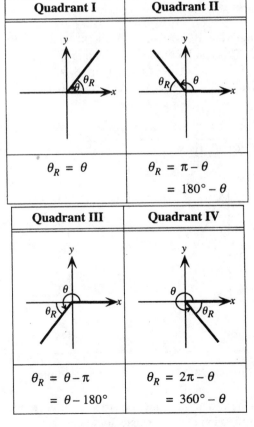

| Quadrant I | Quadrant II |
|---|---|
| $\theta_R = \theta$ | $\theta_R = \pi - \theta$ $= 180° - \theta$ |

| Quadrant III | Quadrant IV |
|---|---|
| $\theta_R = \theta - \pi$ $= \theta - 180°$ | $\theta_R = 2\pi - \theta$ $= 360° - \theta$ |

**Figure 8-19**

Trigonometric functions of angles in terms of reference angles: For any nonquadrantal angle $\theta$, each trigonometric function of $\theta$ has the same absolute value as the same trigonometric function of $\theta_R$. To find a trigonometric function of $\theta$, find the function of $\theta_R$, then apply the correct sign for the quadrant of $\theta$.

**Example 8.13:** Find $\cos\dfrac{3\pi}{4}$.

The reference angle for $\dfrac{3\pi}{4}$, a second quadrant angle, is $\pi - \dfrac{3\pi}{4} = \dfrac{\pi}{4}$. In quadrant II, the sign of the cosine function is negative. Hence, $\cos\dfrac{3\pi}{4} = -\cos\dfrac{\pi}{4} = -\dfrac{1}{\sqrt{2}}$ (see Examples 8.2 and 8.4).

**Example 8.14:** Form a table of the trigonometric functions of 0°, 30°, 45°, 60°, and 90°.

To find the trigonometric functions of 30° and 60°, draw a 30°–60° right triangle. This can be formed by dividing an equilateral triangle in half through one of its vertices (see Figure 8-20). To find the trigonometric functions of 45°, draw an isosceles right triangle (see Figure 8-21).

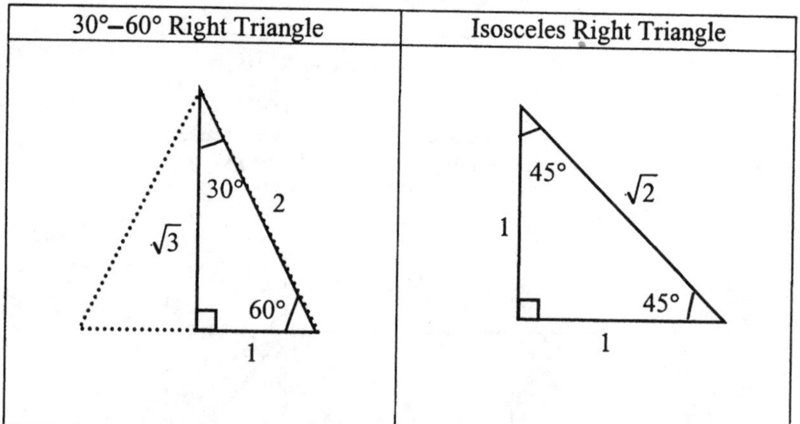

| 30°–60° Right Triangle | Isosceles Right Triangle |
|---|---|
| | |

**Figure 8-20**          **Figure 8-21**

These triangles and the trigonometric functions found in Example 8.2 yield the following table (U stands for undefined):

| $\theta$ (radians) | $\theta$ (degrees) | $\sin\theta$ | $\cos\theta$ | $\tan\theta$ | $\csc\theta$ | $\sec\theta$ | $\cot\theta$ |
|---|---|---|---|---|---|---|---|
| 0 | 0° | 0 | 1 | 0 | U | 1 | U |
| $\pi/6$ | 30° | $1/2$ | $\sqrt{3}/2$ | $\sqrt{3}$ | 2 | $2/\sqrt{3}$ | $1/\sqrt{3}$ |
| $\pi/4$ | 45° | $1/\sqrt{2}$ | $1/\sqrt{2}$ | 1 | $\sqrt{2}$ | $\sqrt{2}$ | 1 |
| $\pi/3$ | 60° | $\sqrt{3}/2$ | $1/2$ | $1/\sqrt{3}$ | $2/\sqrt{3}$ | 2 | $\sqrt{3}$ |
| $\pi/2$ | 90° | 1 | 0 | U | 1 | U | 0 |

# Chapter 9

# TRIGONOMETRIC IDENTITIES AND TRIGONOMETRIC INVERSES

IN THIS CHAPTER:

- ✔ *Inverse Trigonometric Functions*
- ✔ *Trigonometric Identities*
- ✔ *Solving Trigonometric Equations*
- ✔ *Sum, Difference, Multiple, and Half-Angle Formulas*
- ✔ *Triangles*
- ✔ *Polar Coordinates*

## Inverse Trigonometric Functions

The trigonometric functions are periodic, hence they are not one-to-one, and no inverses can be defined for the entire domain of a basic trigonometric function. By redefining each trigonometric function on a carefully chosen subset of its domain, the new function can be specified one-to-one and therefore has an inverse function. The table below shows domains chosen on which each function is one-to-one:

| Function $f(x) =$ | Domain | Range |
|---|---|---|
| $\sin x$ | $\left[-\dfrac{\pi}{2}, \dfrac{\pi}{2}\right]$ | $[-1,1]$ |
| $\cos x$ | $[0,\pi]$ | $[-1,1]$ |
| $\tan x$ | $\left(-\dfrac{\pi}{2}, \dfrac{\pi}{2}\right)$ | $\mathbf{R}$ |
| $\csc x$ | $\left(-\pi,-\dfrac{\pi}{2}\right] \cup \left(0,\dfrac{\pi}{2}\right]$ | $(-\infty,-1] \cup [1,\infty)$ |
| $\sec x$ | $\left[0,\dfrac{\pi}{2}\right) \cup \left[\pi,\dfrac{3\pi}{2}\right)$ | $(-\infty,-1] \cup [1,\infty)$ |
| $\cot x$ | $[0,\pi]$ | $\mathbf{R}$ |

Note that in each case, although the domain has been restricted, the entire range of the original function is retained.

Note also that in each case the restricted domain (sometimes called the *principal domain*) is the result of choice. Other choices might be possible, and in the case of the secant and cosecant functions *no universal agreement exists*. The choice used here is the one most commonly made in elementary calculus texts.

Definitions of inverse trigonometric functions:

1.  Inverse sine $f(x) = \sin^{-1} x$ is defined by $y = \sin^{-1} x$ if and only if $x = \sin y$ with $-1 \leq x \leq 1$ and $-\dfrac{\pi}{2} \leq y \leq \dfrac{\pi}{2}$. The values the function takes on lie in quadrants I and IV.

2.  Inverse cosine $f(x) = \cos^{-1} x$ is defined by $y = \cos^{-1} x$ if and only if $x = \cos y$ with $-1 \leq x \leq 1$ and $0 \leq y \leq \pi$. The values the function takes on lie in quadrants I and II.

3.  Inverse tangent $f(x) = \tan^{-1} x$ is defined by $y = \tan^{-1} x$ if and only if $x = \tan y$ with $x \in \mathbf{R}$ and $-\dfrac{\pi}{2} < y < \dfrac{\pi}{2}$. The values the function takes on lie in quadrants I and IV.

4.  Inverse cosecant $f(x) = \csc^{-1} x$ is defined by $y = \csc^{-1} x$ if and only if $x = \csc y$ with either $x \leq -1$ and $\pi < y \leq \dfrac{3\pi}{2}$ or $x \geq 1$ and

$0 < y \le \dfrac{\pi}{2}$. The values the function takes on lie in quadrants I and III.

5. Inverse secant $f(x) = \sec^{-1} x$ is defined by $y = \sec^{-1} x$ if and only if $x = \sec y$ with either $x \le -1$ and $-\pi \le y < -\dfrac{\pi}{2}$ or $x \ge 1$ and $0 \le y < \dfrac{\pi}{2}$. The values the function takes on lie in quadrants I and III.

6. Inverse cotangent $f(x) = \cot^{-1} x$ is defined by $y = \cot^{-1} x$ if and only if $x = \cot y$ with $x \in R$ and $0 < y < \pi$. The values the function takes on lie in quadrants I and II.

**Example 9.1:** Evaluate (a) $\sin^{-1} \dfrac{1}{2}$; (b) $\sin^{-1}\left(-\dfrac{1}{2}\right)$.

(a) $y = \sin^{-1} \dfrac{1}{2}$ is equivalent to $\sin y = \dfrac{1}{2}$, $-\dfrac{\pi}{2} \le y \le \dfrac{\pi}{2}$. The only solution of the equation on the interval is $\dfrac{\pi}{6}$; hence $\sin^{-1} \dfrac{1}{2} = \dfrac{\pi}{6}$.

(b) $y = \sin^{-1}\left(-\dfrac{1}{2}\right)$ is equivalent to $\sin y = -\dfrac{1}{2}$, $-\dfrac{\pi}{2} \le y \le \dfrac{\pi}{2}$. The only solution of the equation on the interval is $-\dfrac{\pi}{6}$; hence $\sin^{-1} \dfrac{1}{2} = -\dfrac{\pi}{6}$.

**Example 9.2:** Evaluate (a) $\cos^{-1} \dfrac{1}{2}$; (b) $\cos^{-1}\left(-\dfrac{1}{2}\right)$.

(a) $y = \cos^{-1} \dfrac{1}{2}$ is equivalent to $\cos y = \dfrac{1}{2}$, $0 \le y \le \pi$. The only solution of the equation on the interval is $\dfrac{\pi}{3}$; hence $\cos^{-1} \dfrac{1}{2} = \dfrac{\pi}{3}$.

(b) $y = \cos^{-1}\left(-\dfrac{1}{2}\right)$ is equivalent to $\cos y = -\dfrac{1}{2}$, $0 \le y \le \pi$. The only solution of the equation on the interval is $\dfrac{2\pi}{3}$; hence $\cos^{-1} \dfrac{1}{2} = \dfrac{2\pi}{3}$.

The inverse trigonometric functions are also referred to as the arc functions. In this notation:

$$\sin^{-1} x = \arcsin x \quad \cos^{-1} x = \arccos x \quad \tan^{-1} x = \arctan x$$

$$\csc^{-1} x = \operatorname{arccsc} x \quad \sec^{-1} x = \operatorname{arcsec} x \quad \cot^{-1} x = \operatorname{arccot} x$$

**Example 9.3:** Evaluate arctan 1.

$y = \arctan 1$ is equivalent to $\tan y = 1$, $-\dfrac{\pi}{2} < y < \dfrac{\pi}{2}$. The only solution of the equation on the interval is $\dfrac{\pi}{4}$; hence $\arctan 1 = \dfrac{\pi}{4}$.

# Trigonometric Identities

An identity is a statement that two quantities are equal that is true for all values of the variables for which the statement is meaningful.

The basic trigonometric identities are repeated below for reference:

1.  *Pythagorean Identities.* For all $t$ for which both sides are defined:

$$\cos^2 t + \sin^2 t = 1 \quad 1 + \tan^2 t = \sec^2 t \quad \cot^2 t + 1 = \csc^2 t$$

2.  *Reciprocal Identities.* For all $t$ for which both sides are defined:

$$\csc t = \frac{1}{\sin t} \quad \sec t = \frac{1}{\cos t} \quad \cot t = \frac{1}{\tan t}$$

3.  *Quotient Identities.* For all $t$ for which both sides are defined:

$$\tan t = \frac{\sin t}{\cos t} \quad \cot t = \frac{\cos t}{\sin t}$$

4.  *Identities for Negatives.* For all $t$ for which both sides are defined:

$$\sin(-t) = -\sin t \quad \cos(-t) = \cos t \quad \tan(-t) = -\tan t$$
$$\csc(-t) = -\csc t \quad \sec(-t) = \sec t \quad \cot(-t) = -\cot t$$

The basic trigonometric identities are used to reduce trigonometric expressions to simpler form.

**Example 9.4:** Simplify $\dfrac{1 - \cos^2 \alpha}{\sin \alpha}$.

From the Pythagorean identity $1 - \cos^2 \alpha = \sin^2 \alpha$. Hence,

$$\frac{1 - \cos^2 \alpha}{\sin \alpha} = \frac{\sin^2 \alpha}{\sin \alpha} = \sin \alpha$$

To verify that a given statement is an identity, show that one side can be transformed into the other by using algebraic techniques, including simplification and substitution, and trigonometric techniques, frequently including reducing other functions to sines and cosines.

**Example 9.5:** Verify that $\dfrac{\sin t \cos t}{\tan t} = \cos^2 t$ is an identity.

Starting with the left side, the first stop is to reduce to sines and cosines:

$$\frac{\sin t \cos t}{\tan t} = \frac{\sin t \cos t}{\sin t / \cos t} \qquad \text{Quotient Identity}$$

$$= \sin t \cos t \div \frac{\sin t}{\cos t} \qquad \text{Algebra}$$

$$= \sin t \cos t \cdot \frac{\cos t}{\sin t} \qquad \text{Algebra}$$

$$= \cos^2 t \qquad \text{Algebra}$$

If a statement is meaningful yet not true for even only one value of the variable or variables, it is not an identity. To show that it is not an identity, it is sufficient to find one value of the variable or variables that would make it false.

**Example 9.6:** Show that $\sin t + \cos t = 1$ is not an identity.

Although this statement is true for some values of $t$, for example, $t = 0$, it is not an identity. For example, choose $t = \pi/4$. Then

$$\sin \frac{\pi}{4} + \cos \frac{\pi}{4} = \frac{1}{\sqrt{2}} + \frac{1}{\sqrt{2}} = \frac{2}{\sqrt{2}} = \sqrt{2} \neq 1$$

# Solving Trigonometric Equations

Trigonometric equations can be solved by a mixture of algebraic and trigonometric techniques, including reducing other functions to sines and cosines, substitution from known trigonometric identities, algebraic simplification, and so on.

**Example 9.7:** Find all solutions of $\cos t = \dfrac{1}{2}$.

First find all solutions in the interval $[0, 2\pi)$: Start with

$$t = \cos^{-1} \frac{1}{2} = \frac{\pi}{3}$$

Since cosine is positive in quadrants I and IV, there is also a solution in quadrant IV with reference angle $\pi/3$, namely $2\pi - \pi/3 = 5\pi/3$.

Extending to the entire real line, since cosine is periodic with period $2\pi$, all solutions can be written as $\pi/3 + 2\pi n$, $5\pi/3 + 2\pi n$, $n$ any integer.

**Example 9.8:** Find all solutions in the interval $[0,2\pi)$ for $5 \tan t = 3 \tan t - 2$.

First reduce this to a basic trigonometric equation by isolating the quantity $\tan t$.

$$2 \tan t = -2$$
$$\tan t = -1$$

Now find all solutions of this equation in the interval $[0, 2\pi)$. Start with $\tan^{-1} 1 = \pi/4$. Since tangent is negative in quadrants II and IV, the solutions are the angles in these quadrants with reference angle $\pi/4$. These are $\pi - \pi/4 = 3\pi/4$ and $2\pi - \pi/4 = 7\pi/4$.

# Sum, Difference, Multiple, and Half-Angle Formulas

**Sum and Difference Formulas** for sines, cosines and tangents: Let $u$ and $v$ be any real numbers; then

$$\sin(u + v) = \sin u \cos v + \cos u \sin v \qquad \sin(u - v) = \sin u \cos v - \cos u \sin v$$

$$\cos(u + v) = \cos u \cos v - \sin u \sin v \qquad \cos(u - v) = \cos u \cos v + \sin u \sin v$$

$$\tan(u + v) = \frac{\tan u + \tan v}{1 - \tan u \tan v} \qquad \tan(u - v) = \frac{\tan u - \tan v}{1 + \tan u \tan v}$$

**Example 9.9:** Calculate an exact value for $\sin \dfrac{\pi}{12}$.

Noting that $\dfrac{\pi}{12} = \dfrac{\pi}{3} - \dfrac{\pi}{4}$, apply the difference formula for sines:

$$\sin \frac{\pi}{12} = \sin\left( \frac{\pi}{3} - \frac{\pi}{4} \right)$$

$$= \sin \frac{\pi}{3} \cos \frac{\pi}{4} - \cos \frac{\pi}{3} \sin \frac{\pi}{4}$$

$$= \frac{\sqrt{3}}{2} \cdot \frac{1}{\sqrt{2}} - \frac{1}{2} \cdot \frac{1}{\sqrt{2}}$$

$$= \frac{\sqrt{3} - 1}{2\sqrt{2}} = \frac{\sqrt{6} - \sqrt{2}}{4}$$

**Cofunction Formulas** for the trigonometric functions: Let $\theta$ be any real number; then

$$\sin\left(\frac{\pi}{2}-\theta\right)=\cos\theta \quad \cos\left(\frac{\pi}{2}-\theta\right)=\sin\theta \quad \tan\left(\frac{\pi}{2}-\theta\right)=\cot\theta$$

$$\csc\left(\frac{\pi}{2}-\theta\right)=\sec\theta \quad \sec\left(\frac{\pi}{2}-\theta\right)=\csc\theta \quad \cot\left(\frac{\pi}{2}-\theta\right)=\tan\theta$$

**Double-Angle Formulas** for sines, cosines, and tangents: Let $\theta$ be any real number; then

$$\sin 2\theta = 2\sin\theta\cos\theta \quad \cos 2\theta = \cos^2\theta - \sin^2\theta \quad \tan 2\theta = \frac{2\tan\theta}{1-\tan^2\theta}$$

**Half-Angle Identities** for sine and cosine: Let $u$ be any real number; then

$$\sin^2 u = \frac{1-\cos 2u}{2} \quad \cos^2 u = \frac{1+\cos 2u}{2}$$

**Half-Angle Formulas** for sine, cosine, and tangent: Let $A$ be any real number; then

$$\sin\frac{A}{2}=(\pm)\sqrt{\frac{1-\cos A}{2}} \quad \cos\frac{A}{2}=(\pm)\sqrt{\frac{1+\cos A}{2}} \quad \tan\frac{A}{2}=(\pm)\sqrt{\frac{1-\cos A}{1+\cos A}}$$

$$=\frac{1-\cos A}{\sin A}$$

$$=\frac{\sin A}{1+\cos A}$$

The sign of the square root in these formulas cannot be specified in general; in any particular case it is determined by the quadrant in which $A/2$ lies.

**Example 9.10:** Given $\cos\theta = \frac{2}{3}$, $\frac{3\pi}{2} < \theta < 2\pi$, find $\sin\frac{\theta}{2}$ and $\cos\frac{\theta}{2}$.

Use the half-angle formulas for sine and cosine. Since $\frac{3\pi}{2} < \theta < 2\pi$, dividing all sides of this inequality by 2 yields $\frac{3\pi}{4} < \frac{\theta}{2} < \pi$. Therefore $\frac{\theta}{2}$ lies in quadrant II and the sign of $\sin\frac{\theta}{2}$ is to be chosen positive, while the sign of $\cos\frac{\theta}{2}$ is to be chosen negative.

$$\sin\frac{\theta}{2} = +\sqrt{\frac{1-\frac{2}{3}}{2}} = \sqrt{\frac{1}{6}} \quad \cos\frac{\theta}{2} = -\sqrt{\frac{1+\frac{2}{3}}{2}} = -\sqrt{\frac{5}{6}}$$

## Triangles

The conventional notation for a triangle $ABC$ is shown in Figure 9-1.

| Right Triangle | Acute Triangle | Obtuse Triangle |
|---|---|---|
| B, β, c, a, α, γ, C, A, b | B, β, c, a, α, γ, C, A, b | B, β, c, a, α, γ, C, A, b |

**Figure 9-1**

A triangle that contains no right angles is called an *oblique triangle*. The six parts of the triangle $ABC$ are the three sides $a$, $b$, and $c$, together with the three angles $\alpha$, $\beta$, and $\gamma$.

*Solving a triangle* is the process of determining all the parts of the triangle. In general, given three parts of a triangle, including at least one side, the other parts can be determined. (Exceptions are cases where two possible triangles are determined or where no triangle can be shown to be consistent with the given data.)

With right triangles one part is known from the outset to be an angle of 90°. Given either two sides, or one side and one of the acute angles, the other parts can be determined using the definitions of the trigonometric functions for acute angles, the Pythagorean Theorem, and the fact that the sum of the three angles in a plane triangle is 180°.

**Example 9.11:** Given a right triangle $ABC$ with $c = 20$ and $\alpha = 30°$, solve the triangle.

Here it is assumed that $\gamma = 90°$.
Solve for $\beta$:
  Since $\alpha + \beta + \gamma = 180°$, $\beta = 180° - \alpha - \gamma = 180° - 30° - 90° = 60°$.
Solve for $a$:

In the right triangle $ABC$, $\sin \alpha = \dfrac{a}{c}$, hence $a = c \sin \alpha = 20 \sin 30° = 10$.
Solve for $b$:
  From the Pythagorean theorem, $c^2 = a^2 + b^2$; hence

$$b = \sqrt{c^2 - a^2} = \sqrt{20^2 - 10^2} = \sqrt{300} = 10\sqrt{3}$$

  Oblique triangles are solved using the law of sines and the law of cosines.

**Law of Sines:** In any triangle, the ratio of each side to the sine of the angle opposite that side is the same for all three sides:

$$\frac{a}{\sin \alpha} = \frac{b}{\sin \beta} \qquad \frac{a}{\sin \alpha} = \frac{c}{\sin \gamma} \qquad \frac{b}{\sin \beta} = \frac{c}{\sin \gamma}$$

**Law of Cosines:** In any triangle, the square of any side is equal to the sum of the squares of the other two sides, diminished by twice the product of the other two sides and the cosine of the angle included between them:

$$a^2 = b^2 + c^2 - 2bc \cos \alpha$$
$$b^2 = a^2 + c^2 - 2ac \cos \beta$$
$$c^2 = a^2 + b^2 - 2ab \cos \gamma$$

  When solving triangles, the law of cosines is most often used when one angle and two sides are known. Otherwise, the law of sines is usually more appropriate.

**Example 9.12:** Solve the triangle $ABC$, given $\alpha = 23.9°$, $\beta = 114°$, and $c = 82.8$.

  Since two angles are given the law of sines it is the most appropriate formula to use.
Solve for $\gamma$:
$\alpha + \beta + \gamma = 180°$, $\gamma = 180° - \alpha - \beta = 180° - 23.9° - 114° = 42.1°$.

Solve for $a$ (using the law of sines):

$$\frac{a}{\sin\alpha}=\frac{c}{\sin\gamma}; \text{ hence } a=\frac{c\sin\alpha}{\sin\gamma}=\frac{82.8\sin 23.9^\circ}{\sin 42.1^\circ}=50.0$$

Solve for $b$ (using the law of sines again):

$$\frac{b}{\sin\beta}=\frac{c}{\sin\gamma}; \text{ hence } b=\frac{c\sin\beta}{\sin\gamma}=\frac{82.8\sin 114^\circ}{\sin 42.1^\circ}=113$$

## Polar Coordinates

A *polar coordinate system* (Figure 9-2) specifies points in the plane in terms of directed distances $r$ from a fixed point called the *pole* and angles $\theta$ measured from a fixed ray (with initial point the pole) called the *polar axis*. The polar axis is the positive half of a number line, drawn to the right of the pole.

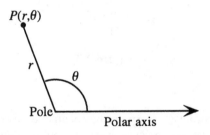

**Figure 9-2**

For any point $P$, $\theta$ is an angle formed by the polar axis and the ray connecting the pole to $P$, and $r$ is the distance measured along this ray from the pole to $P$. For any ordered pair $(r,\theta)$, if $r$ is positive, take $\theta$ as an angle with vertex the pole and initial side the polar axis, and measure $r$ units along the terminal side of $\theta$. If $r$ is negative, measure $|r|$ units along the ray directed opposite to the terminal side of $\theta$. Any pair with $r = 0$ represents the pole. In this manner every ordered pair $(r,\theta)$ is represented by a unique point.

**Example 9.13:** Graph the points specified by $(3,\pi/3)$ and $(-3,\pi/3)$ (Figure 9-3).

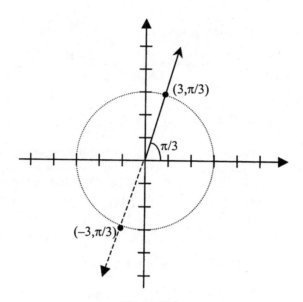

**Figure 9-3**

The polar coordinates of a point are not unique, however. Given point $P$, there is an infinite set of polar coordinates corresponding to $P$, since there are an infinite number of angles with terminal sides passing through $P$.

**Example 9.14:** List four alternative sets of polar coordinates corresponding to the point $P(3,\pi/3)$.

Adding any multiple of $2\pi$ yields an angle coterminal with a given angle; hence $(3,7\pi/3)$ and $(3,13\pi/3)$ are two possible alternative polar coordinates. Since $\pi + \pi/3 = 4\pi/3$ has terminal side the ray opposite to $\pi/3$, the coordinates $(-3,4\pi/3)$ and $(-3,10\pi/3)$ are further alternative polar coordinates for $P$.

If a polar coordinate system is superimposed upon a Cartesian coordinate system, as in Figure 9-4, the transformation relationships below hold between the two sets of coordinates.

If $P$ has polar coordinates $(r,\theta)$ and
Cartesian coordinates $(x,y)$, then

$$x = r\cos\theta \quad y = r\sin\theta$$

$$r^2 = x^2 + y^2$$

$$\tan\theta = \frac{y}{x} \quad (x \neq 0)$$

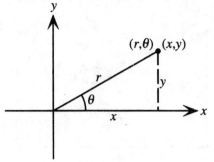

**Figure 9-4**

**Example 9.15:** Convert $(6,2\pi/3)$ to Cartesian coordinates.

Since $r = 6$ and $\theta = 2\pi/3$, applying the transformation relationship yields

$$x = r\cos\theta = 6\cos 2\pi/3 = -3 \quad y = r\sin\theta = 6\sin 2\pi/3 = 3\sqrt{3}$$

Thus the Cartesian coordinates are $\left(-3, 3\sqrt{3}\right)$.

**Example 9.16:** Convert $(-5, -5)$ to polar coordinates with $r > 0$ and $0 \leq \theta \leq 2\pi$.

Since $x = -5$ and $y = -5$, applying the transformational relationships yields

$$r^2 = x^2 + y^2 = (-5)^2 + (-5)^2 = 50 \quad \tan\theta = \frac{y}{x} = \frac{-5}{-5} = 1$$

Since $r$ is required to be positive, $r = \sqrt{50} = 5\sqrt{2}$. Since the given point lies in quadrant III, $\theta = 5\pi/4$. The polar coordinates that satisfy the given conditions are $\left(5\sqrt{2}, 5\pi/4\right)$.

Any equation in the variables $r$ and $\theta$ may be interpreted as a polar coordinate equation. Often $r$ is specified as a function of $\theta$.

# Chapter 10
# SEQUENCES AND SERIES

IN THIS CHAPTER

✔ Sequences
✔ Series
✔ Series Identities
✔ Arithmetic Sequences and Series
✔ Geometric Sequences and Series
✔ Binomial Theorem

## Sequences

A *sequence* is a function with domain the natural numbers (*infinite sequence*) or some subset of the natural numbers from 1 up to some larger number (*finite sequence*). The notation $f(n) = a_n$ is used to denote the range elements of the function: the $a_1, a_2, a_3, \ldots$ are called the first, second, third, etc., terms of the sequence, and $a_n$ is referred to as the $n$th term. The independent variable $n$ is referred to as the index. Unless otherwise specified a sequence is assumed to be an infinite sequence.

**Example 10.1:** Write the first four terms of the sequence specified by $a_n = 2n$.

$a_1 = 2 \cdot 1, a_2 = 2 \cdot 2, a_3 = 2 \cdot 3, a_4 = 2 \cdot 4$. The sequence would be written $2 \cdot 1, 2 \cdot 2, 2 \cdot 3, 2 \cdot 4, \ldots$, or $2, 4, 6, 8, \ldots$.

**Example 10.2:** Write the first four terms of the sequence specified by $a_n = (-1)^n$.
$a_1 = (-1)^1, a_2 = (-1)^2, a_3 = (-1)^3, a_4 = (-1)^4$. The sequence would be written $(-1)^1, (-1)^2, (-1)^3, (-1)^4 \ldots$, or $-1, 1, -1, 1, \ldots$.

Given the first few terms of a sequence, a common exercise is to determine the $n$th term, that is, a formula which generates all the terms. In fact such a formula is not uniquely determined, but in many cases a simple one can be developed.

**Example 10.3:** Find a formula for the $n$th term of the sequence 1, 4, 9, 16, ....
Notice that the terms are all perfect squares, and the sequence could be written $1^2, 2^2, 3^2, 4^2, \ldots$. Thus the $n$th term of the sequence can be given as $a_n = n^2$.

A sequence is defined *recursively* by specifying the first term and defining later terms with respect to earlier terms.

**Example 10.4:** Write the first four terms of the sequence defined by $a_1 = 3, a_n = a_{n-1} + 7, n < 1$.

For $n = 1, a_1 = 3$.
For $n = 2, a_2 = a_{2-1} + 7 = a_1 + 7 = 3 + 7 = 10$.
For $n = 3, a_3 = a_{3-1} + 7 = a_2 + 7 = 10 + 7 = 17$.
For $n = 4, a_4 = a_{4-1} + 7 = a_3 + 7 = 17 + 7 = 24$.
The sequence can be written 3, 10, 17, 24, ....

# Series

A *series* is the indicated sum of the terms of a sequence. Thus if $a_1, a_2, a_3, \ldots, a_m$ are the $m$ terms of a finite sequence, then associated with the sequence is the series given by $a_1 + a_2 + a_3 + \ldots + a_m$. Series are often written using summation notation:

$$a_1 + a_2 + a_3 + \ldots + a_m = \sum_{k=1}^{m} a_k$$

Here $\Sigma$ is called the *summation symbol*, and $k$ is called the *index of summation* or just the index. The right-hand side of this definition is read, "the sum of the $a_k$, with $k$ going from 1 to $m$."

**Example 10.5:** Write in expanded form: $\displaystyle\sum_{k=1}^{5}\frac{1}{k^2}$.

Replace $k$, in turn, with the integers from 1 to 5 and add the results:

$$\sum_{k=1}^{5}\frac{1}{k^2}=\frac{1}{1^2}+\frac{1}{2^2}+\frac{1}{3^2}+\frac{1}{4^2}+\frac{1}{5^2}=1+\frac{1}{4}+\frac{1}{9}+\frac{1}{16}+\frac{1}{25}=\frac{5269}{3600}$$

## Series Identities

$$\sum_{k=1}^{n}a_k+\sum_{k=1}^{n}b_k=\sum_{k=1}^{n}(a_k+b_k) \qquad \sum_{k=1}^{n}a_k-\sum_{k=1}^{n}b_k=\sum_{k=1}^{n}(a_k-b_k)$$

$$\sum_{k=1}^{n}ca_k=c\sum_{k=1}^{n}a_k \qquad \sum_{k=1}^{n}c=cn$$

$$\sum_{k=1}^{n}k=\frac{n(n-1)}{2} \qquad \sum_{k=1}^{n}k^2=\frac{n(n+1)(2n+1)}{6}$$

$$\sum_{k=1}^{n}k^3=\frac{n^2(n+1)^2}{4} \qquad \sum_{k=1}^{n}k^4=\frac{n(n+1)(2n+1)(3n^2+3n-1)}{30}$$

## Arithmetic Sequences and Series

A sequence of numbers $a_n$ is an *arithmetic sequence* if successive terms differ by the same constant, called the *common difference*. Thus $a_n-a_{n-1}=d$ and $a_n=a_{n-1}+d$ for all terms of the sequence. It can be proved that for any arithmetic sequence, $a_n=a_1+(n-1)d$.

An *arithmetic series* is the indicated sum of the terms of a finite arithmetic sequence. The notation $S_n$ is often used, thus, $S_n=\displaystyle\sum_{k=1}^{n}a_k$. For an arithmetic series,

$$S_n=\frac{n}{2}(a_1+a_n) \qquad S_n=\frac{n}{2}\left[2a_1+(n-1)d\right]$$

**Example 10.6:** Write the first 6 terms of the arithmetic sequence 4, 9, .... Since the sequence is arithmetic, with $a_1=4$ and $a_2=9$, the common difference $d$ is given by $a_2 - a_1 = 9 - 4 = 5$. Thus, each term can be found from the previous term by adding 5, hence the first 6 terms are 4, 9, 14, 19, 24, 29.

**Example 10.7:** Find the sum of the first 20 terms of the sequence of the previous example.

To find $S_{20}$, either of the formulas for an arithmetic series may be used. Since $a_1 = 4$, $n = 20$, and $d = 5$ are known, the second formula is more convenient:

$$S_n = \frac{n}{2}\big[2a_1 + (n-1)d\big]$$

$$S_{20} = \frac{20}{2}[2 \cdot 4 + (20-1)5] = 1030$$

# Geometric Sequences and Series

A sequence of numbers $a_n$ is called a *geometric sequence* if the quotient of successive terms is a constant, called the *common ratio*. Thus $a_n \div a_{n-1} = r$ or $a_n = ra_{n-1}$ for all terms of the sequence. It can be proved that for any geometric sequence, $a_n = a_1 r^{n-1}$.

A *geometric series* is the indicated sum of the terms of a geometric sequence. For a geometric series with $r \neq 1$, $S_n = a_1 \dfrac{1 - r^n}{1 - r}$.

**Example 10.8:** Write the first 6 terms of the geometric sequence 4, 6, ... .

Since the sequence is geometric, with $a_1 = 4$ and $a_2 = 6$, the common ratio $r$ is given by $a_2 \div a_1 = 6 \div 4 = 3/2$. Thus, each term can be found from the previous term by multiplying by 3/2; hence the first 6 terms are 4, 6, 9, 27/2, 81/4, 243/8.

**Example 10.9:** Find the sum of the first 8 terms of the sequence of the previous example.

Use the sum formula with $a_1 = 4$, $n = 8$, $r = 3/2$:

$$S_n = a_1 \frac{1 - r^n}{1 - r}$$

$$S_8 = 4\frac{1 - (3/2)^8}{1 - (3/2)} = \frac{6305}{32}$$

## Binomial Theorem

Binomial expansions, that is, binomials or other two-term quantities raised to integer powers, are of frequent occurrence. If the general binomial expression is $a + b$, then the first few powers are given by:

$$(a+b)^0 = 1$$
$$(a+b)^1 = a+b$$
$$(a+b)^2 = a^2 + 2ab + b^2$$
$$(a+b)^3 = a^3 + 3a^2b + 3ab^2 + b^3$$

Many patterns have been observed in the sequence of expansions of $(a + b)^n$. For example:
1. There are $n + 1$ terms in the expansion of $(a + b)^n$.
2. The exponent of $a$ starts in the first term as $n$, and decreases by 1 in each succeeding term down to 0 in the last term.
3. The exponent of $b$ starts in the first term as 0, and increases by 1 in each succeeding term up to $n$ in the last term.

The *Binomial Theorem* gives the expansion of $(a + b)^n$. In its most compact form this is written as follows:

$$(a+b)^n = \sum_{r=0}^{n} \binom{n}{r} a^{n-r} b^r$$

The symbols $\binom{n}{r}$ are called the binomial coefficients, defined as:

$$\binom{n}{r} = \frac{n!}{r!(n-r)!}.$$

For natural numbers $n$, $n!$ (pronounced *n factorial*) is defined as the product of the natural numbers from 1 up to $n$. Then

$$1! = 1 \quad 2! = 1 \cdot 2 = 2 \quad 3! = 1 \cdot 2 \cdot 3 = 6 \quad 4! = 1 \cdot 2 \cdot 3 \cdot 4 = 24$$

and so on. Separately, 0! is defined to equal 1.

**Example 10.10:** Find the fifth term in the expansion of $(a + b)^{16}$.

Here $n = 16$ and $j + 1 = 5$, thus $j = 4$ and the term is given by

$$\binom{n}{j} a^{n-j} b^j = \binom{16}{4} a^{16-4} b^4 = \frac{16!}{4!(16-4)!} a^{12} b^4 = 1820 a^{12} b^4$$

# *Index*

Absolute value, 3, 24–26
Algebra of functions, 47–50
Algebraic functions and their
   graphs, 54–70
Analytic geometry, 39–43
Angles, 96–103
Asymptotes, 66–70
Axioms for the real number sys-
   tem, 2

Binomial theorem, 120

Cartesian coordinate system, 39
Circle, unit, 87–89
Common ratio, 119
Completing the square, 15
Complex numbers, 3
Conic sections, 78–86
Cosines, 92–93, 112

Direct variation, 20

Elimination method of solving,
   29–32, 37–38
Ellipses, 82–84
Equations, 13–26
Exponential functions, 71–73,
   75–77
Exponents, 8–9

Factoring, 6–8, 15
FOIL method, 6
Formulas
   cofunction, 110
   double-angle, 110

   half-angle, 110
   sum and difference, 109
Functions, 43–50

Graphical method of solving, 29–
   30, 36–38
Graphs of trigonometric functions, 92–96

Hyperbolas, 84–85

Identities
   negatives, 91
   Pythagorean, 91
   quotient, 91
   reciprocal, 91
   series, 118
   trigonometric, 91, 107–08
Imaginary numbers, 3
Inequalities, 3, 21–24
Inverse trigonometric functions,
   104–07
Inverse variation, 20

Joint variation, 20

Laws
   associative, 2
   commutative, 2
   cosine, 112
   distributive, 2
   negatives, 2
   quotients, 2
   sine, 112
   zero factor, 2

Like terms, 5
Linear equations, 14–15
Linear functions, 54–55
Linear systems, 29–32
Loci, 78–79
Logarithmic functions, 73–77

Nonlinear systems of equations, 36–38
Numbers
    integers, 1
    irrational, 2
    natural, 1
    rational, 2
    real, 1
    sets of, 1–2
Number systems, 1–12

Order of operations, 4

Parabolas, 79–82
Parametric equations, 26
Partial fraction decomposition, 32–36
Point-slope form, 55
Polar coordinates, 113–15
Polynomial functions, 59–60
Polynomials, 4–6, 61–63

Quadratic equations, 15–17
Quadratic functions, 56–59

Radical equations, 17–18
Radical expressions, 11–12
Rational expressions, 9–11
Rational functions, 66–70

Secant and cosecant, 94–95
Sequences and series, 116–20
Series, 117–19
Sets of numbers, 1–2
Sines, 92–93, 112
Slope-intercept form, 55
Square root property, 15
Standard form, 55
Substitution method of solving, 29–32, 36–38
Systems of equations and partial fractions, 27–38

Tangent and cotangent, 94–95
Theorems
    binomial, 120
    corollary, 64
    Descartes's rule of signs, 64
    intermediate value, 64
    zeros, 63–65
Transformations and graphs, 50–53
Triangles, 111–13
Trigonometric equations, 108–09
Trigonometric functions, 87–103
Trigonometric identities and inverses, 104–15

Unit circle, 87–89
Unlike terms, 5

Variation, 19–21
Vertical line test, 45